QUILLING
ROUND THE YEAR

QUILLING
ROUND THE YEAR

Beautiful Quilled Creations
for Every Season

RACHEL WARRILLOW

HERBERT PRESS
LONDON · OXFORD · NEW YORK · NEW DELHI · SYDNEY

HERBERT PRESS
Bloomsbury Publishing Plc
50 Bedford Square, London, WC1B 3DP, UK
29 Earlsfort Terrace, Dublin 2, Ireland

Bloomsbury, Herbert Press and the Herbert Press logo are
trademarks of Bloomsbury Publishing PLC

First published in Great Britain in 2025

A catalogue record for this book is available from the
British Library.

Library of Congress Cataloguing-in-data has been applied
for.

ISBN: 9781789942354; eBook: 9781789942347

2 4 6 8 10 9 7 5 3 1

Design by Jeremy Goldie Graphic Design

Printed and bound in China by RR Donnelley APS

FSC
www.fsc.org

MIX
Paper | Supporting
responsible forestry
FSC® C144853

To find out more about our authors and books, visit
www.bloomsbury.com and sign up for our newsletters

Page 1 image: A monochrome mandala.
Page 2 image: A black, blue and white guitar.
This page: A beautiful cat.
Opposite: A honey bee.

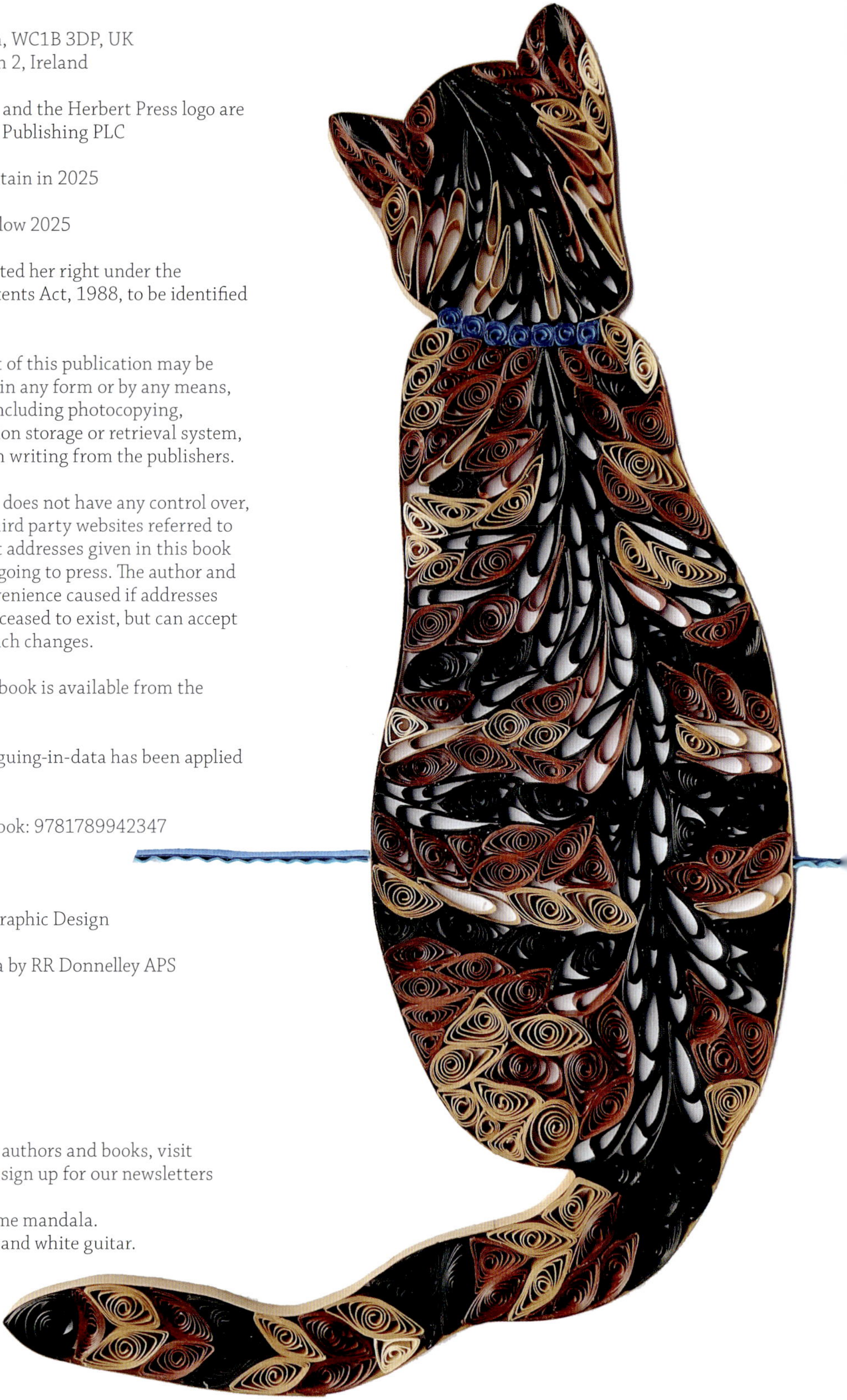

CONTENTS

Introduction

The world of quilling is a wonderful place to spend time. Welcome to a land of colour, pattern and design, where this inexpensive and accessible paper craft will help you to escape from real life for a moment, taking time for yourself to take a breath and slow down, all while creating stunning, beautiful, cute or quirky designs.

It really is amazing just how much you can do with simple cut strips of paper. In this book, I will show you some basic building blocks of quilling to get you started and show you that with even a small number of techniques and skills you can create a never-ending selection of designs.

One of the joys of quilling is that it is so easy to get started and even the simplest design can be effective and impactful.

Left: My first ever solo design.

Below: My desk at home.

Smaller, quicker projects are perfect to create greeting cards, gift tags, magnets or hanging decorations. You can then build on these to create beautiful wall art of any size or shape.

While I have a dedicated area for quilling, it's a compact and portable craft that can be done anywhere. Very little equipment or space is needed!

What is quilling?

Quilling, which is also sometimes called paper filigree, uses narrow strips of paper which we curl, shape or fold (perhaps even a combination of these) before gluing them on their edges to make fabulous designs.

The widths of the paper strips can vary, and you can introduce a range of tools and techniques to create different effects.

With the paper raised up from the page you get a wonderful play of light, reflection, pattern and colour.

Why quilling?

This is a question I get asked a lot!

I used to quill as a little girl, way back in the 1980s, when it was only just coming back to public attention, thanks in a huge way to the newly formed UK Quilling Guild.

While I've always been an active crafter, I didn't do a great deal at all for a long time. Then in 2020, when many of us had more time at our disposal, I rediscovered my long-lost love of quilling.

Artists such as Yulia Brodskaya and Justine Kuran were raising the profile, updating it and adding a new vibrance for the modern quiller. I was inspired to have another go, and have not looked back since.

Above: The repetitive action of making coils can be very therapeutic. You will find me quilling even before I know what I will use the shapes and colours for!

In my mid-thirties I was diagnosed with autism spectrum disorder (ASD). Suddenly, so much of my life made sense to me! Crafting has always been a way to help me recharge and find some escapism when things felt hard, but it's also a way to connect with the world. Since my diagnosis I have realised how important it has always been, but also how it has great potential to help others too, whether neurodiverse or not.

Quilling, in particular, is a craft that has such a calming effect but is fun too; it offers so much in such a simple way. I love colour and pattern, so that element really speaks to me. I find the repetitive nature of rolling the coils of paper meditative and soothing; a wonderful way to calm a busy mind.

Why quilling round the year?

The more you quill, the more you start to see the world in quilling shapes! Inspiration is all around us, everywhere we go.

A couple of years ago I relocated from Birmingham, where I had lived with my husband for eight years, to a village at the top of a hill in beautiful Calderdale, West Yorkshire. That move from urban to rural surroundings was such a huge change; I started to notice the weather and the changing seasons so much more than ever before.

My mission is to encourage people to enjoy this fabulous craft, and by taking elements of the four seasons it will hopefully provide a wonderful starting point with something for everyone to relate to. From plants and flowers, food, animals, seasonal decorations, edible treats – there really is so much inspiration to infuse into our quilling all year round.

In each chapter you will find a quick project that will take an hour or two, two medium projects for when you have a bit longer to spend on your craft, and one more involved project that you can really get your teeth into.

The mandala design in Part 5 represents all four seasons, and will be a wonderful combination of all the skills you will be developing within the other projects in the book.

If you are completely new to quilling, the quicker projects will be a great starting point for you, with the longer projects there for when you are ready. You will see as you go through that the techniques will often be repeated as elements in several designs, helping you practise and improve your skills as the perfect foundation to quilling anything your heart desires in the future.

The Quilling Guild

We are very lucky to have The Quilling Guild, a UK registered charity, to promote, protect and publicise the world of quilling. It is run by a group of volunteers, and I am very honoured to say I have recently joined their ranks as a committee member.

Quilling is certainly not a recent invention and on its website the Guild has a fascinating feature on the history of quilling which explains that many of the techniques we still use today are thought to have been originally practised in Ancient Egypt.

The Quilling Guild is an international organisation with membership open to everyone with a love for quilling, from complete beginners to the very experienced. It's a wonderful way to connect with others and to keep in touch with news and innovations from members around the world through social media and a regular magazine, helping to preserve this fabulous craft for many generations to come!

The Quilling Guild

Far left: Quilled designs can make beautiful hanging decorations. There are special gilded edge papers which can make them extra beautiful.

Below: Quilling doesn't have to be complicated. Colour, light and shade can have wonderful effects.

Therapeutic and mindful

Taking time out of our busy schedules and having a go at a mindful activity such as quilling can bring so many benefits. It can give you respite from the stressful world we live in. It can be an unofficial therapy, giving you space to build up your strength to carry on and with the added benefit of something tangible at the end – a wonderful, quilled design to gift or display.

It has always been my haven when times are tough, and I would love more people to experience the joy it brings me.

I have met so many wonderful people in the quilling world and my own online community, The Quirky Quillers Collective, are such a wonderful, supportive, friendly group of people. All connected by strips of paper and what we do with them! To have that balance between taking part in a solitary activity and then using it to connect with others is really special.

From my customers, colleagues, friends and followers, I hear time and time again how much quilling means to them. I can't wait to see how much it might mean to you too!

Right: This design was created as a kit for Craft for Cats, by Cats Protection. Proceeds from sales of this kit raised over £25,000 for the UK charity.

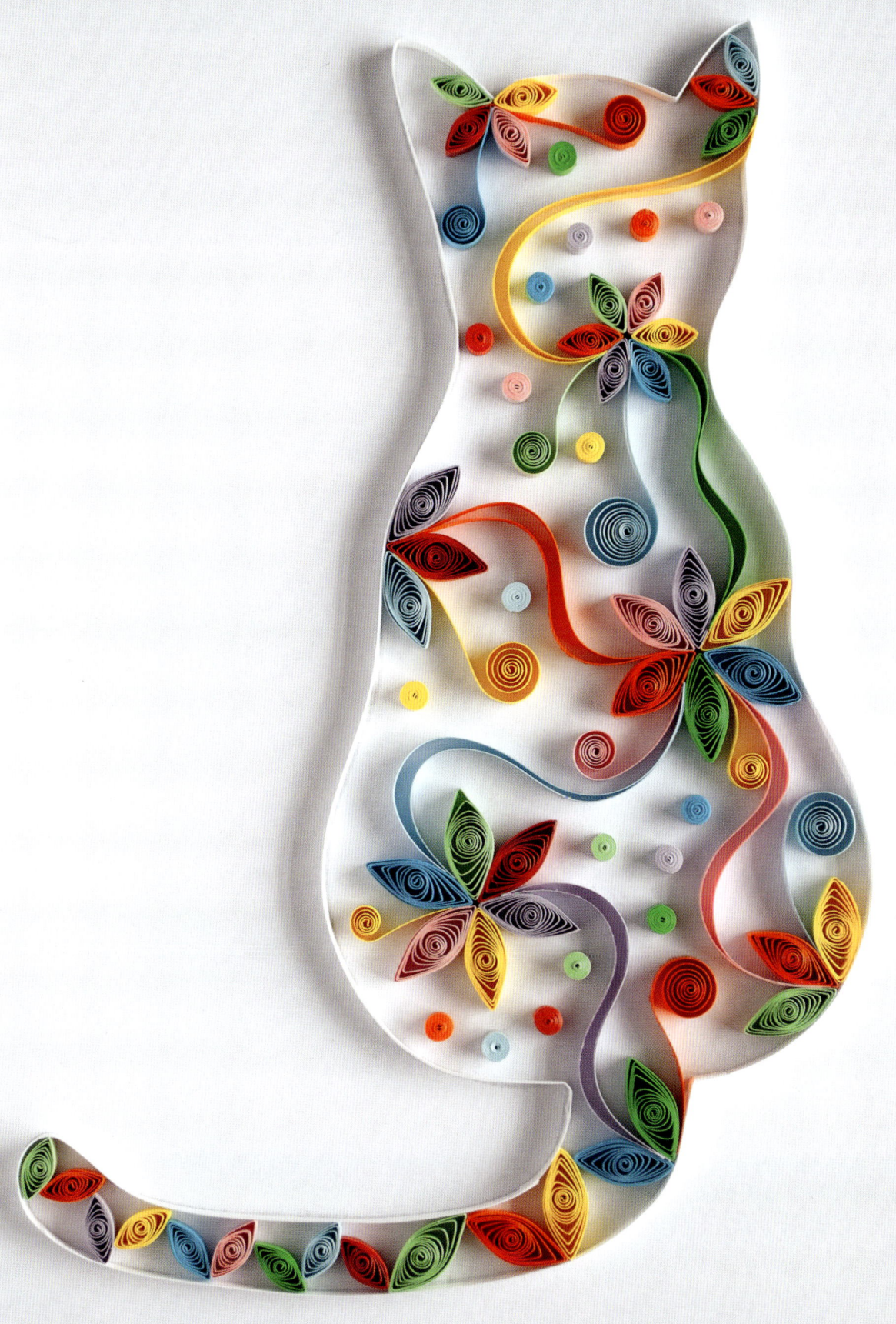

Far left: Decorated letters are always popular, and perfect for a personalised gift.

Left: Empty space can be just as important as filled space in quilled designs.

Tree of Life – another tree composition to show how designs can be adapted and changed.

Right: Mandalas can be any size, colour or design, providing endless ways to play with your favourite techniques and coils.

Before we begin

I know as crafters we can strive for this idea of 'perfection' in the things we make. I'd like to ask you to be gentle with yourself while you are quilling. After all, if we wanted something the same as everyone else has, we'd buy something manufactured by machines.

Please don't worry if your creation doesn't look exactly like the one in the photo. That's a good thing! Something of you will always show itself through your fingers when you craft, and that's part of the magic of the process.

However many times I create one of my own designs, they are all slightly different.

So by all means, make adjustments wherever you feel like it. If a bit doesn't fit, miss it out. If there's a gap, fill it with something. These are my instructions, but this is your design now.

Happy quilling!

Rachel x

Tools and Materials

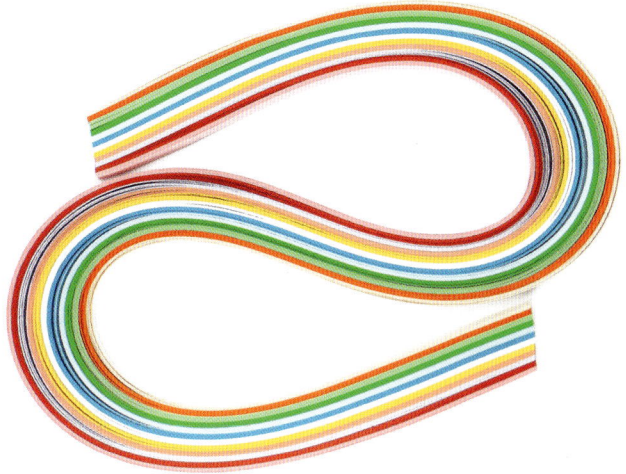

Paper for quilling

With quilling becoming an ever-more popular craft, there is now a plentiful, but also somewhat confusing, array of quilling paper out there to choose from. A lot of it comes down to personal preference. Do be aware, though, that if you use poor quality paper, it will affect the quality of your quilling.

Quilling paper comes in a huge variety of colours too, in mixed colour packs and single colours. Plus there are speciality papers with metallic edges or graduated colours. Play and experiment to see which you like the best.

Use any colours at all for your creations; the ones used in the book are simply suggestions.

The most commonly used width of paper for quilling is 3 mm and this is the width used in the book, unless stated otherwise. There are also 1.5 mm, 2 mm, 5 mm and 10 mm widths available.

Left: Whatever space you have to craft in, whether a dedicated room or a corner of a table, surround yourself with anything that will entice you to spend time there. and inspire your creativity.
© Sarah Mason

A good, heavy-weight paper
or card is best for quilling onto.
Anything from 220 gsm will be great,
even for the larger designs. Watercolour paper
or mixed media paper is also good to use.

Slotted quilling tools

While you can quill just using your hands, I find a quilling tool is a very
handy investment, and this is the way I teach. It makes things so much easier,
especially when you're just starting out.

The quilling tools available today are so much better than they used to be,
but do be careful as not all of them are made equal. It's surprising how much
difference a quilling tool can make to the designs you create.

There are two main types: the standard quilling tool and the super-fine tip
quilling tool.

The standard tool is bigger, stronger and perfect for larger scale quilling, or
for nervous beginners and children.

The super-fine tool is, like the name suggests, finer. This one gives a lovely
finish to your quilling. Because the tip is more delicate, the hole in the centre
of your quilling is smaller and improves the appearance, especially if you are
going for smaller details in your designs.

Glue and glue applicator

While PVA glue is often recommended for quilling, I have found over time
that some PVAs can be a bit watery and slow to stick.

I use, and therefore always recommend, a tacky glue rather than a straightfor-
ward PVA. It is still non-toxic and clear-drying – which is the most important
factor – but it is quicker to stick, which can make a big difference.

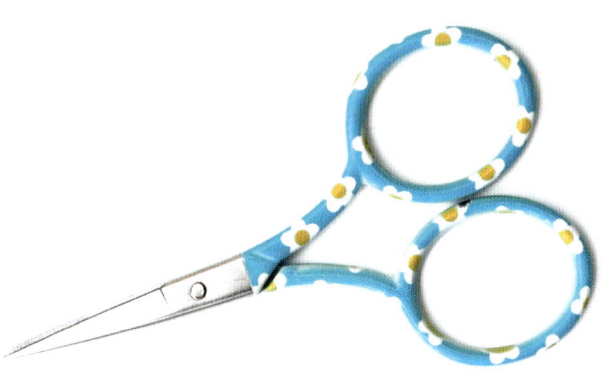

Scissors

I like to use a small pair of embroidery scissors, as they have a nice point and come in lots of patterns! But any small scissors will do. Remember, whenever you are cutting paper it will blunt the scissors, so don't use the same scissors you use for fabric or thread.

Fringing scissors

These are very sharp, very pointed scissors used for cutting small, fine details, such as when we need to do some fringing. They come with a cap to protect the point and are not suitable for children to use.

In this book, while we don't do any fringing, these scissors, with a super-pointed end, are really handy for cutting out your quilled designs on their backing paper if you want to hang them or add them to a larger composition. The sharp points allow you to get into all the nooks and crannies.

Paper crimper

This is a really simple-to-use but very effective piece of equipment. Simply feed the paper through the cogs and turn the handle on the top. The paper comes out the other side crimped, giving you a lovely new texture to work with.

Circle sizer

This can be very handy if you want your coils to be very uniform in size. It also has a regular ruler along the edge for measuring your strips.

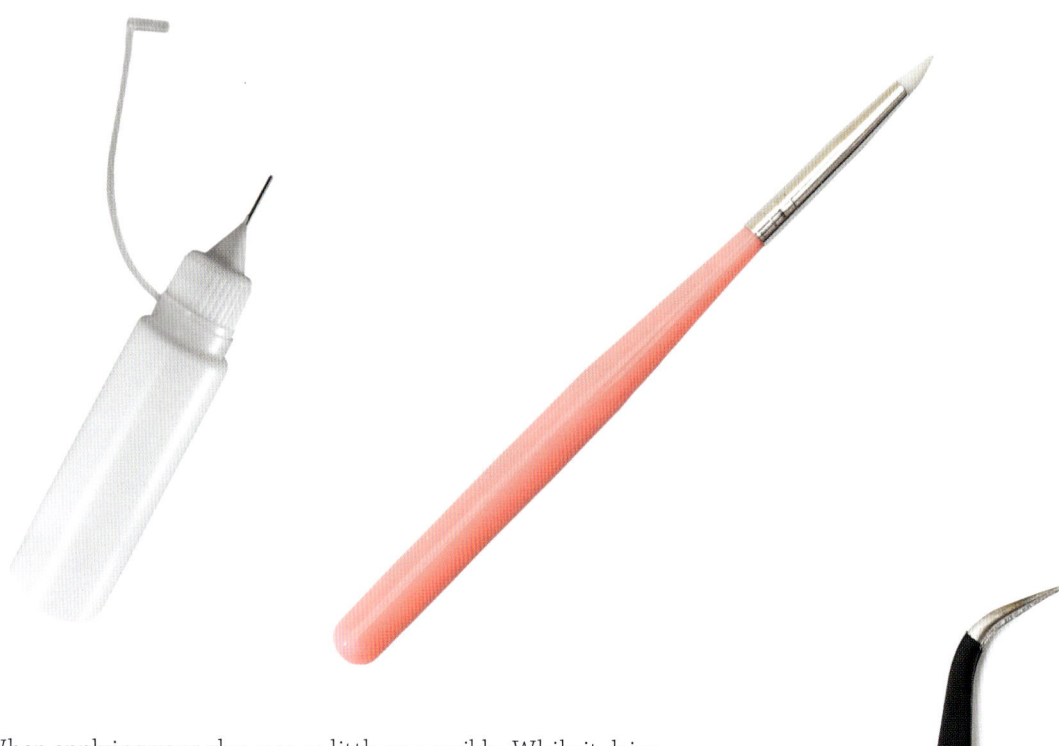

When applying your glue, use as little as possible. While it dries clear, you still don't want lots of messy blobs of glue spoiling your work. Using an applicator with a fine tip helps you control how much glue you apply.

Acrylic brush

This is an optional extra, but I find it really handy to use this to wipe away any glue residue that you don't want. It can get into really fine nooks and crannies and is easy to wipe clean. Alternatively, you can use a regular small paintbrush or your tweezers instead.

Tweezers

Tweezers with a fine point are also really handy and can make things so much easier.

Their angled, fine tip means you can get hold of your coils, place things with control, and avoid gluey fingers.

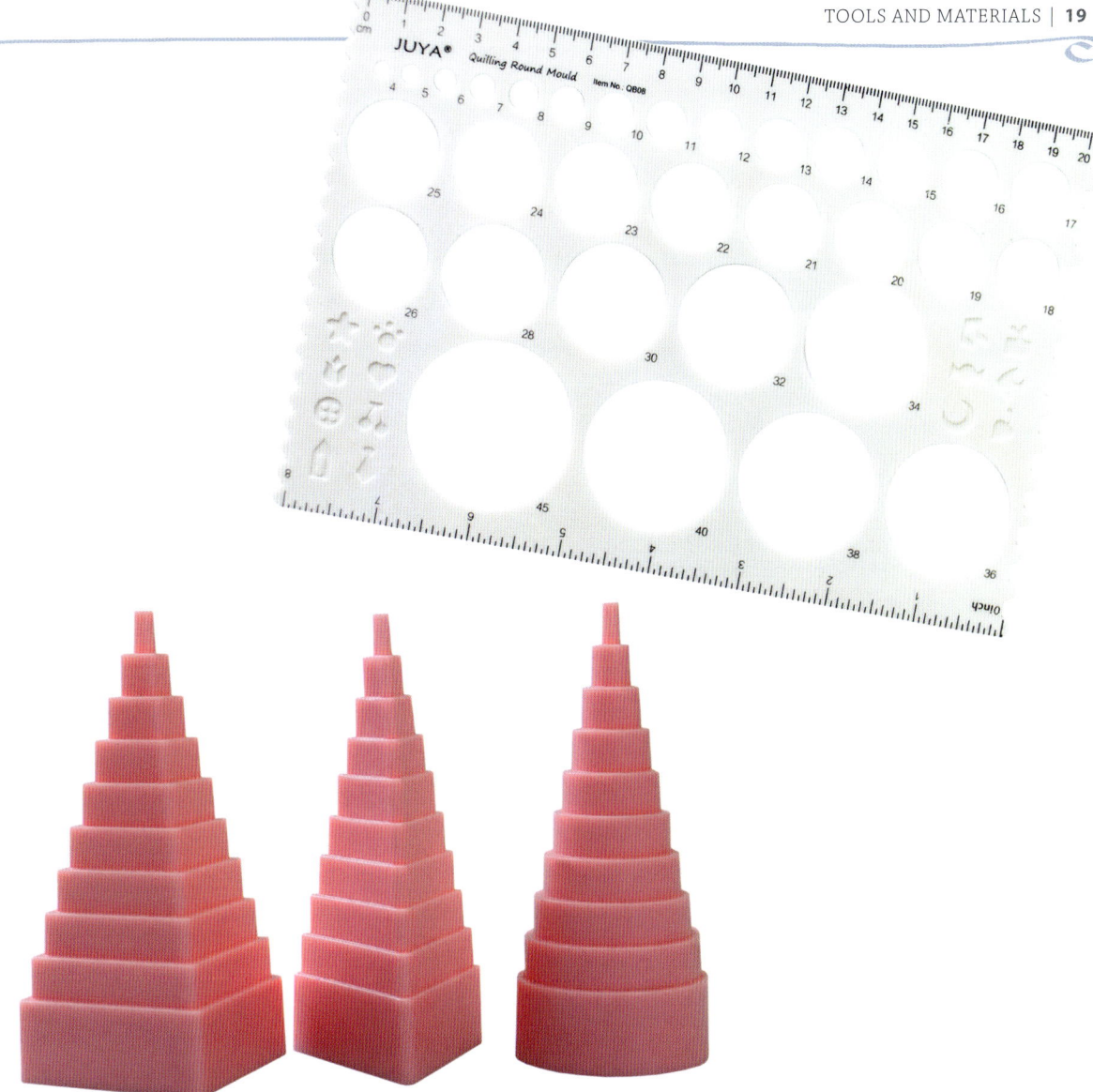

Border makers

Border makers generally come in sets of different shapes, but they are all used in the same way – by wrapping the strip around your chosen shape. When you slide it off the tool, you have a shape that you can use in your designs, whether you quill inside or outside of the outline. This is the one we use for the projects in this book.

If you don't have specially made border makers, you can use items you already have around the house, particularly for the circular shape. Look for something cylindrical like pens, dowels, bottles, etc., for different sizes. Just ensure you will be able to slide the paper off whatever you are using, once you have wound it round and glued the end.

Techniques

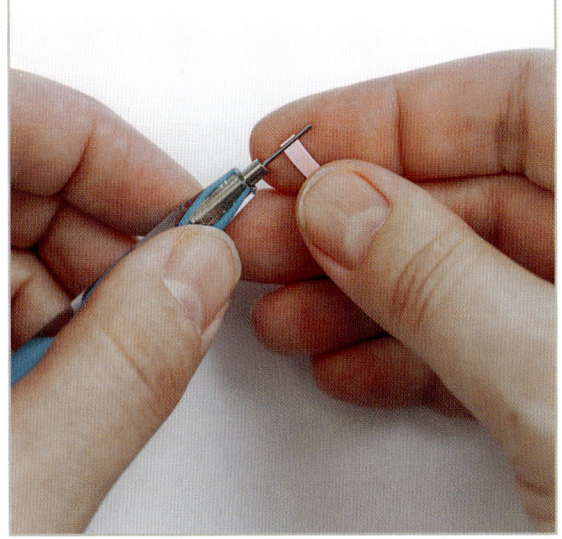

see how it affects the coils you end up with – but consistency is key if you are making something where you want the coils to be roughly the same.

Guide the paper with your index finger as you go, and try to get the layers evenly on top of each other.

When you have finished rolling, you should be able to slide the coil off the tool easily.

Let it go, and the coil will relax and open up, OR keep hold of it and glue the end down, and you have a tight coil.

Using a slotted quilling tool

Hold the quilling tool in one hand and feed the strip of paper held in your other hand between the tongs of the tool.

There's no need to thread it like a needle; this would be really hard, especially with a super-fine tip quilling tool. Slide it in over the top, wiggling your quilling tool until it slides in.

You want the paper to just be peeking out the other side – not too far – so when you start rolling the tool, the paper will stay in place.

Keep your hands nice and relaxed.

You don't need to worry about keeping it taut – you can experiment with different tensions and

Closed loose coils

This is a term you will see a lot in this book as it is so useful, the real building block of quilling.

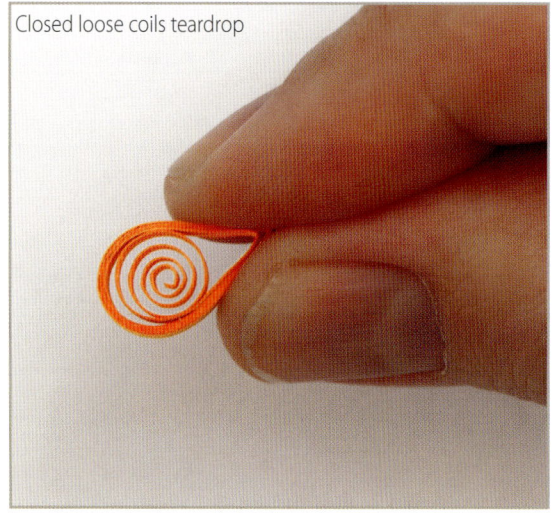

Closed loose coils teardrop

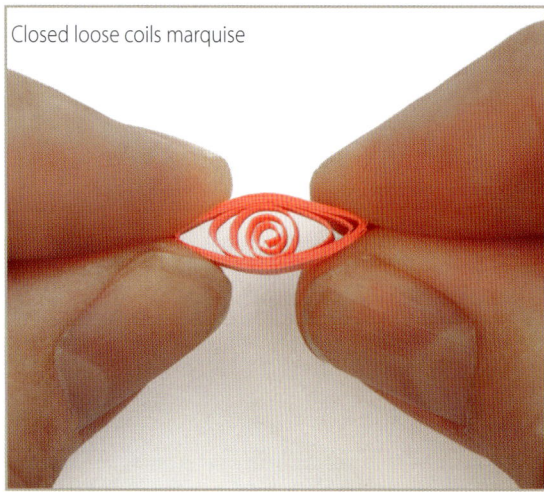

Closed loose coils marquise

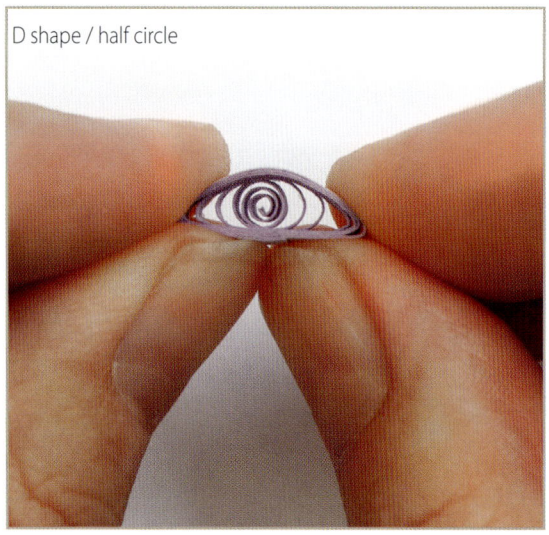

D shape / half circle

Roll the length of paper that you need on your quilling tool, slide it off the tool and let go. It will relax and unravel a little bit, creating a loose coil. Dab a little bit of glue at the end of the strip and stroke it down in place to seal it.

From this basic coil, you can create many different shapes:

Teardrop

Start with a closed loose coil.

Using finger and thumb, pinch a fold into one end to make a teardrop shape.

Marquise

Start with a closed loose coil.

This time, pinch two folds at the same time, one at each end to make a marquise.

D shape / half circle

Starting with a closed loose coil, use the pads of your thumb to make the straight side, and stroke down the curved sides to make two points.

Open coils

Open coils have a curly end with a tail. I find it easiest to coil the whole of the strip and then unwind to make the tail. You can also use your nail or scissors to change the shape of the tail end.

Open coils

S scrolls

S scrolls

Start by coiling from one end of your strip towards the middle.

Then go to the other end of the strip and coil in the opposite direction, to meet the other half of the coil.

For several projects in this book we use these coils as a method to fill space. For this purpose, it really doesn't matter if the two ends are different sizes; in fact that is often useful. By placing these within a border, you can fill spaces more quickly than simply using closed loose coils, and if you have a smaller coil at one end of your S scroll, that might be the perfect piece to fit into a smaller gap.

Heart scrolls

Fold your strip of paper in half so you have a 'V' shape. Take one side and coil inwards towards the point (**a**).

Heart scrolls

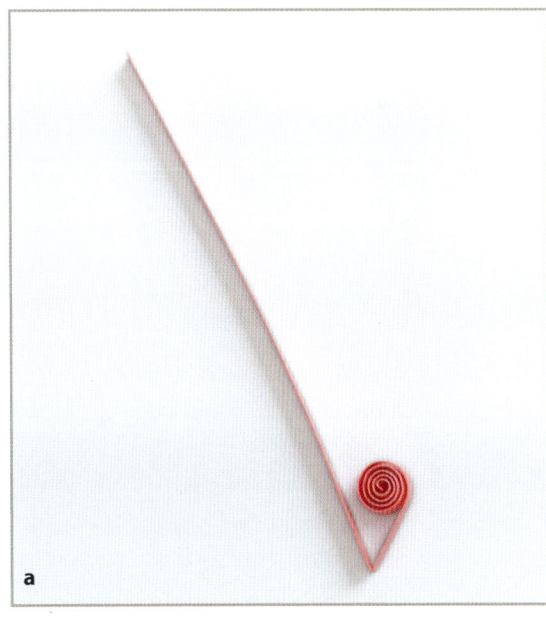

a

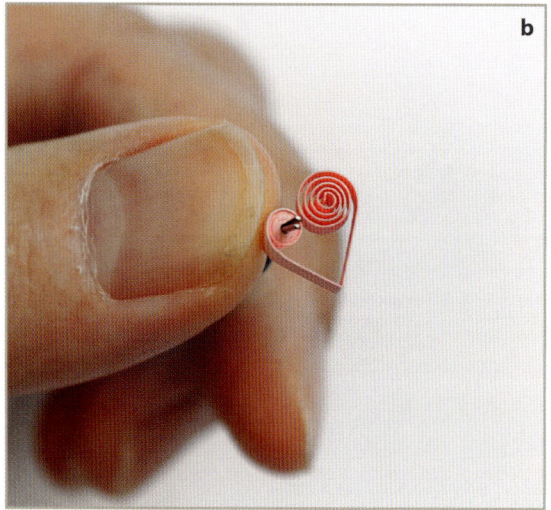

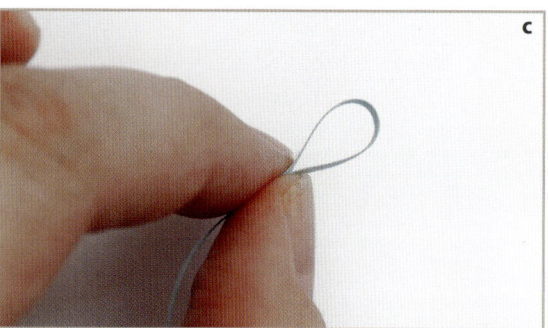

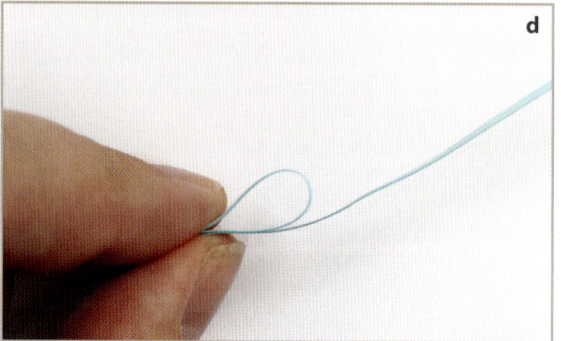

Then do the same with the other side (**b**). The trickiest part is to get the two sides the same. My top tip for this is that when your second side is still tightly wound it should just reach the bottom of your opened coil. You can always adjust them when you come to glue them down if they are still a little uneven.

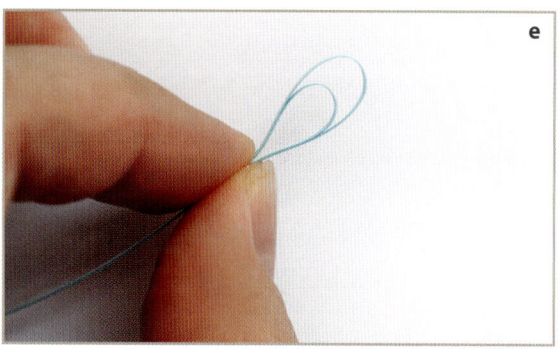

Wheatears

At one end of your strip make a small loop (**c**).

Where the end of the loop meets the body of the paper, fold the paper over so the end is tucked into the fold (**d**). The paper is going in the same direction.

At the base of the loop, fold the paper over and bring the strip over the top of your first loop to create a second (**e**).

Keep going in the same direction, to make as many loops as you wish (**f**). You can vary the gaps between the loops each time. If you want to make the loops very regular, you can use the tines of a comb to wind them around (see p. 31).

Tight coils

Tight coils

Roll the length of paper that you need onto your quilling tool, and this time when you slide it off the tool, don't let go! Keep hold of it while you put some glue on the end of the strip and stick down. This is a tight coil.

To add multiple colours, glue different strips together first before coiling.

Making borders

Using a border maker is very simple and really effective.

You take a strip of paper, or several joined together depending on the size of the shape you need, and wrap them around your chosen step on the tool.

If it needs to be a rigid shape then you can apply glue the whole length of paper as you wind it around.

If you want some flexibility, for example using a circular border maker and shaping into a teardrop, only apply glue at the start and end of the paper strips.

Making borders

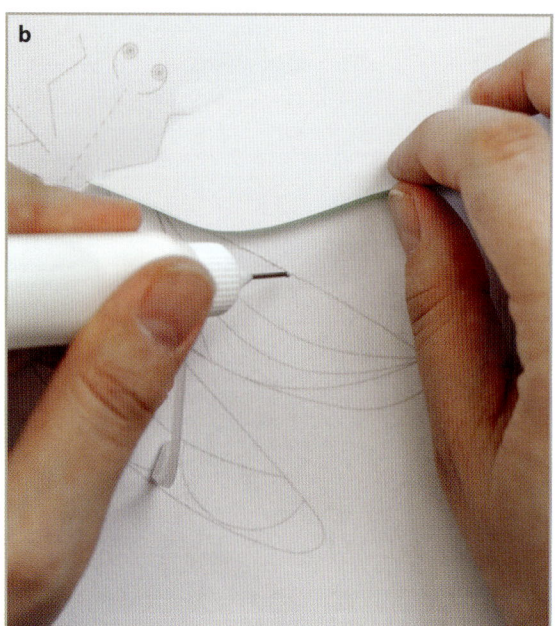

On-edge quilling

The most important thing to consider for on-edge quilling is the quality of your paper strips. If you use thin, poor quality paper you will really struggle to get clean lines.

I use Japanese Tant paper for both traditional coils and my on-edge. While the weight of the paper is not particularly high (116 to 120 gsm), it is slightly textured making it stronger and more robust.

If you are using regular quilling paper (around 120 gsm), you might find it helps to double it up.

I never use pins or corkboards with my quilling; I always quill directly onto the backing paper. I generally draw out my design and use a lightbox.

You will find it really helps to use a good quality, quick drying tacky glue, and apply it as sparingly as possible.

The more you can shape the paper strip before applying it to your backing card, the easier you will find this technique.

Work in short sections. To start with, apply the glue directly to the paper strip (**a**) and place down on your line. Wipe away any excess glue. Hold it for a moment to allow it to dry.

Then move the strip to one side and apply dots of glue to the next section before placing the strip back on the line (**b**). Take your time, adding your on-edge quilling bit by bit.

To turn a sharp corner, use your pointed tweezers to pinch the paper where you need to make a turn. Push the paper around the tweezers to give you a nice sharp corner (**c**). Continue as before in your new direction.

Slow and steady wins the race for this technique!

Applying glue

Less is more! You will be amazed how little glue you really need to secure your papers. I never dip any paper into a pool of glue, as it's so hard to control how much you get on the paper and it's usually too 'blobby'.

a

Rather than measure lots of different paper lengths with a ruler, when I'm designing a project I usually stick to cutting my strips in half, quarters, eighths, etc.

The paper I use is 39 cm long, but I realise that not everybody will start with the same length of paper as I do.

Throughout this book I will give the measurements of the length of paper strips, but if you use the same length of paper as me, they work out as the following:

Full strip = 39 cm
$^1/_2$ strip = 19.5 cm
$^1/_3$ strip = 13 cm
$^1/_4$ strip = 9.75 cm (rounded up to 10 cm)
$^1/_8$ strip = 4.8 cm (rounded up to 5 cm)

If you use an applicator with a fine tip, it really helps you control how much glue you apply. Also, keep it tipped up while not in use. This means the glue stays right at the tip, meaning less squeezing for you and making it easier on your hands; it's also much less likely to dry up. In addition, you can keep a bit of damp sponge at the bottom to help prevent the glue drying out between uses.

For your coils, apply little dots of glue (**a**), a little around the edge and a little in the middle, and then place down on your design; that's really all that is needed.

An acrylic brush is also very handy for wiping away glue from anywhere you don't want it!

Part 1:

Spring

Each season has its own highlights, of course, but spring is my absolute favourite of all. Seeing the natural world start to come to life again after a long winter is such an uplifting time.

The first flowers emerging, fighting their way up through the cold earth, are such a symbol of hope and new life, and to see some colour appearing is so joyful.

The trees in blossom are fleeting, again adding colour to the world in a celebration of the sun getting stronger and days getting longer.

Spring showers, especially where I live in the north of England, are only to be expected, but can create dramatic skies – and beautiful rainbows.

The colours I have used for these spring creations are fresh and clean. Pastels are perfect for early spring, with the colours gradually getting bolder and stronger as the season moves on.

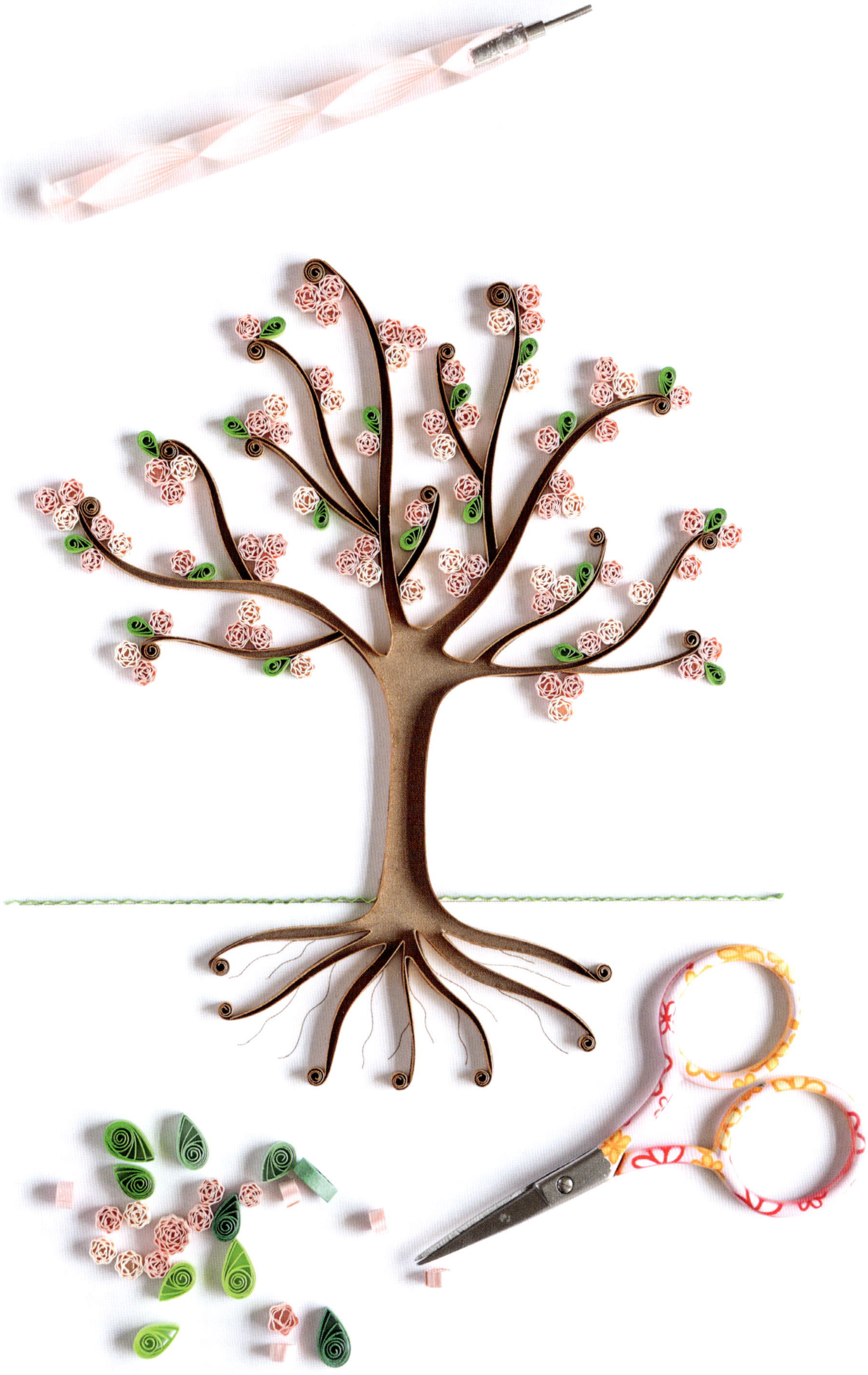

Celandine

One colour that I really associate with the spring is yellow. From celandines and dandelions to laburnums, it's a colour that wants to be noticed against the wonderful green of spring.

This little flower is inspired by the celandine, and one I can imagine coming across while walking in woodland. It's so delicate, yet so strong to be one of the first on the scene in the season of new life!

To make the petals in this project I have demonstrated a technique using a fine-tooth comb. If you don't have one to hand, you can always make a very similar flower using teardrop coils instead.

The flower can take pride of place on its own as a gift tag, or be part of a floral arrangement on a card or framed picture.

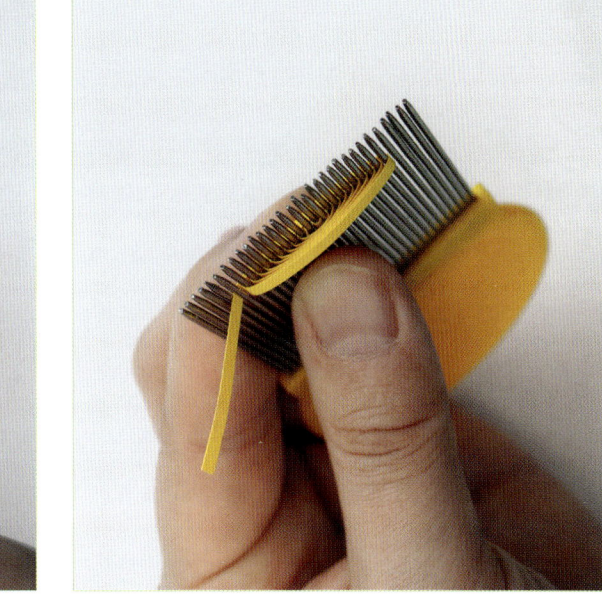

Step 1.

Take a 39 cm length strip and make a tiny loop at one end. Thread this loop onto the centre tooth of the comb.

Bring the strip up between the next tooth of the comb to one side.

Step 2.

Using your starting loop as your centre point, go side to side, winding the strip down between the teeth on one side, and up on the next, not leaving any gaps.

Keep going until you reach the end of your strip of paper.

Step 3.

Glue down the end and then very gently slide the coil off the comb.

Step 4.

Take your petal, and using pointed tweezers, pinch in the middle. Then push the two ends around towards each other to make a 'U' shape.

Step 5.

Keep pushing until the points meet. Then while pinching together, glue another strip of paper (the same or a contrasting colour) to one side of the petal. Wrap this strip around the petal twice, trim off any excess, and glue down. This will hold the shape of the petal together.

Step 6.

Repeat steps 1 to 5 until you have eight petals that look like this.

Step 7.

Make a tight coil from a 10 cm strip for the centre. Glue this down onto your backing card. Arrange the petals around it to ensure even spacing before sticking anything down.

Depending on the texture and thickness of your paper strips you may only fit seven petals rather than eight. See which works best for your coils first, before committing to your chosen number.

THE SMALLER FLOWER (FOR THE MANDALA ON PAGE 108)

The smaller flower is made in exactly the same way, using the following dimensions:

Petals – 19.5 cm strips

Flower centre – 5 cm strip

Bunny Rabbit

Often associated with Easter and springtime, I wanted to create a fun and cute design of a bunny rabbit for you.

I always remember being out and about as a little girl and coming across a rabbit on the path in front of us. It would pause, and we would hear it thump a warning to others with its hind leg that strangers were approaching. I knew for this project that I wanted the feet to be a prominent feature!

Perhaps when you've created this rabbit you might like to try adding Easter eggs to your design, or making a whole family of bunnies?

Step 1.

Take two full length strips (39 cm) and glue together end to end. Use the 7th step on the border maker, or your alternative, to make a circle approximately 36 mm in diameter. This will be the body.

Use one full length strip and the 4th step of the border maker to create a circle approximately 20 mm in diameter. This will be the head.

As you glue them down onto your backing card, use your fingers to shape them a little, giving the body a more oval form, and the head a narrower top and wider bottom.

Step 2.

Put two strips (each 39 cm long) of your second colour through a crimper then glue together end to end. Coil gently, securing the end down without letting it unravel. Shape into a gentle teardrop and glue down in the chest area as shown.

Step 3.

Make a number of S scrolls using 10 cm lengths of paper.

In this case these are fillers to make the brown fur, so don't worry about the size of the coils or if they are uneven. If you have small gaps that's fine, but you can always use a single coil too, if you need to fill an obvious gap that an S scroll won't fit.

Step 4.

Fill the whole of the head and body with your S scrolls.

Step 5.

Make two closed loose coils from 10 cm strips of crimped paper in your second colour. Don't allow the coils to unravel, just coil gently and glue the end down. These are the cheeks.

Make one closed loose coil in pink, and another in the same colour as the fur, this time in 5 cm strips, for the nose and chin and pinch them into a triangular shape.

Glue these four elements to each other first, and then you can decide where you want them to be on the head, before securing in place.

Step 6.

Make the following elements for the feet:

- Two circles made on a border maker, one strip on the 4th step (20 mm in diameter), shaped into gentle teardrops.

- Six closed loose coils in pink from 5 cm strips for the toes.

- Two closed loose coils using a 19.5 cm strip in pink, shaped into a teardrop and then wrapped in a 39 cm strip of your main colour.

Step 7.

Glue the elements of the feet into the outer teardrops as shown, fixing the pads of the feet first and then the toes.

Make two more closed loose coils from 19.5 cm strips in your main colour. Shape them into teardrops and then shape around your thumb to create more of a curve. These will be your rabbit's front paws.

Step 8.

Glue all four paws into place.

Step 9.

To make the ears, start with a 9 cm strip of pink and make a wheatear with four loops. Then join a 19.5 cm strip of brown to your pink wheatear and make four more loops.

Glue the ears into place and add googly eyes (I've used 4 mm eyes).

If you wish, you can add little whiskers to your bunny as a finishing touch. For these I have taken a short length of strip, around 1 cm, and folded in half to make a 'V' shape.

Glue these in place on either side of the cheeks to finish your bunny rabbit.

Blossom Tree

I absolutely love it when the trees bloom with blossom; it seems to happen so suddenly and adds such a pop of colour wherever they are found. I have one in our little garden in Yorkshire, so that was the inspiration for this project.

I have used pink for my blossom but of course you could choose white or yellow, or a glorious raspberry – whatever your favourite would be!

For this design you could use the template from page 126 or 127, but create designs for trees at other times of the year. A glorious mixture of greens for the summer, perhaps some apples too? A riot of copper and orange colours and falling leaves for autumn, and perhaps a snowy landscape for a winter tree.

Step 1.

Line the branches and the trunk of the tree with on-edge quilling.

Top tip, to help you with the branches: start at the top end of a branch, turning the paper in your quilling tool just two or three times to create a tiny coil. This gives you something to hold onto when you're gluing it down, and gives it a bit of extra stability.

That way, when you edge the second line, you can also tuck the cut end into the coil to get a nice clean start for your second side.

On this section I have gone down to the crook of the branch and up the next one, so at the top of that section I have a cut end. Then I can start the next line with a tiny coil and do the same thing in reverse.

Step 2.

To creat the blossoms, take lengths of just 5 cm and put them through a paper crimper to give them a textured effect before gently coiling them and gluing the ends down without letting them unwind. This gives a lovely impression of petals.

Place them on the branches at random, in groups of ones, twos and threes. I have used two shades of pink for mine.

Step 3.

Keep going until you are happy with the number of flowers on your tree and feel they are evenly spaced. Then glue down.

Step 4.

Using a nice spring green, run a strip through the crimper and add some 'grass' to the ground line.

Cut some lengths of 5 cm and make closed loose coils, pinched into teardrops. Glue into place, again at random, to give some new leaves to the tree.

Rainbow in the Clouds

A rainbow is always a wonderful sight to see, isn't it? I know it's a natural phenomenon, but there's always a hint of magic for me – perhaps from stories of pots of gold that are reported to be found where they meet the ground?

They are also such a symbol of hope, not to mention the glorious spectrum of colours.

As well as using a range of colours, this design also uses a lovely range of different styles of coil to create a really decorative, as well as colourful, rainbow.

I have put clouds at the end of mine, but perhaps you would like to change yours to add that elusive pot of gold instead?

Trace or print out the outline of the rainbow, either in light grey for quilling directly onto (p. 129) or black lines for using with a lightbox (p. 128).

Depending on the way you like to work, you can make all your coils first and then glue them down, or make the coils as you go along.

For this design, ALL the coils use the same length of strip (10 cm). For all closed loose coils used in this design, you are aiming for a diameter of around 8 mm.

I have given you guidelines for the numbers of pieces needed; you might find you need one or two fewer or extra, depending on your spacing.

Row 1, violet: seven tight coils, six marquises. Place these right on the inside line of the rainbow template, alternating between the two shapes.

Row 2, indigo: 12 S scrolls, set in two rows – the first directly on top of the marquises, the second row then fits into the gaps created by the first row.

Row 3, blue: 34 teardrops glued in pairs to make 17 hearts.

Glue these so they bump right up against the S scrolls below, with the point of one heart fitting closely into the top of the next one.

Row 4, green:
17 closed loose coils left as circles. Pop one round coil in the dip between each of the hearts on the previous row.

Then fix 17 tight coils in between each circle on the grey line of the template.

Row 5, yellow:
18 marquises, glued together in pairs, joined at the point. Place a pair of marquise coils in every other gap between the tight coils below, floating just above.

For each of the pairs of marquise coils, create a tight coil (nine required). Place these tight coils so they are nestled in the dip between the two marquises.

An additional nine marquises need to be placed in the remaining gaps, floating in the space, with the tips just crossing over the grey line of the template.

Row 6, orange: ten teardrops, nine to be placed next to the tight coils on the previous row, with the point facing away, and one to sit separately on the left of the design (which will eventually connect to the cloud).

nine S scrolls, aiming for equal sizes, each side placed in the gaps between your teardrops.

Row 7, red: 20 teardrops glued into pairs to make heart scrolls, and placed upside down over the points of the teardrops on the previous row.

20 marquises, glued into pairs, joined at the tips so they flare outwards. Stick these down in the gaps between the upside down hearts.

ten tight coils glued inside the pairs of marquises.

That's the rainbow itself completed; now we need some clouds.

The clouds

Step 1.

Print out or trace the cloud shapes and cut them out.

Place a strip of grey quilling paper along the bottom edge of the cloud.

Make a selection of larger and smaller open coils. Place a few of the larger ones around the outside, nice and close to define the edges.

To give you a guideline, for the open coils in the example, I might use a 22 cm length strip, coiling it up with a quilling tool, leaving a tail of around 4 cm before letting it uncurl.

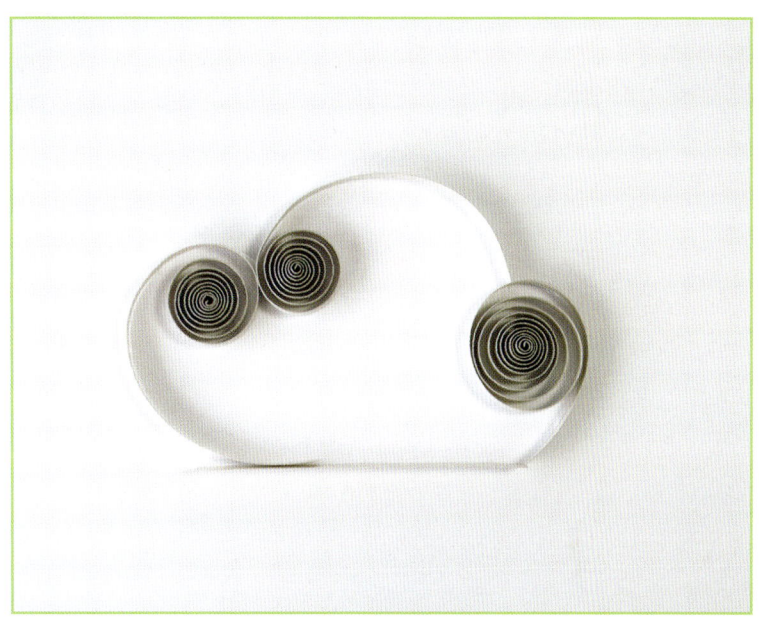

Step 2.

Build up your design using a variety of open coils and as many as you like. There is no set pattern these need to follow. Repeat on the second cloud.

The clouds are going to be raised in front of the rainbow, so if you have any spare coils left over glue three or four to the back of your cloud, not too close to the edge.

Step 3.

Glue the clouds in place at the ends of your rainbow to finish your design.

© Sarah Mason

Part 2: # Summer

To me, the summer always conjures up images of gardens in full bloom, flowers opening up to the sun's rays and butter-flies and dragonflies adding even more colour and movement.

It's a time to get together with friends, to be outside and to luxuriate in any good weather we are lucky enough to have!

For summer the colours are bright and vibrant to reflect the heat of the summer sun, warm days and holidays.

Project 5.

Butterflies

I have always been fascinated by butterflies, since visiting Tropical World in Leeds as a little girl and seeing them fly all around us.

You really can have fun with this design. It's perfect for complete beginners and you can choose any colours that you fancy.

This simple little butterfly is a multi-purpose design. It can be used on its own for greeting cards, gift tags or magnets, or added to a larger design, perhaps a butterfly visiting a bunch of flowers, for instance? If you glue the coils to each other as you go, rather than gluing down onto a backing paper, you could also make lots of them to hang from threads to make a mobile.

This is also the emblem for summer included in the mandala project in Part 5. In the main step-by-step instructions I have guided you through with slightly larger proportions. The sizes for the smaller butterfly follow at the end, and it is made in exactly the same way.

Step 1.

Make a closed loose coil from a 19.5 cm length of paper and shape it into a teardrop.

Then with another strip of the same length, glue the end by the point of your coil. Wrap this second colour around your teardrop, folding it over the point. Wrap right to the end, and glue down.

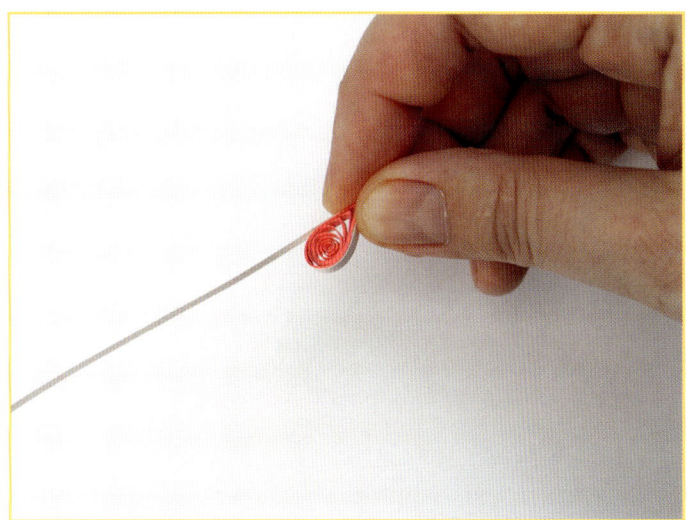

Step 2.

For the wings you will need four teardrops in total, all wrapped in a second colour.

You might wish to have all four wings in the same colour, or you may wish to have the upper wings in one set of colours and the lower wings reversed or a completely different set of colours.

Whatever you choose, bear in mind that you want the sets of wings as a mirror image of each other.

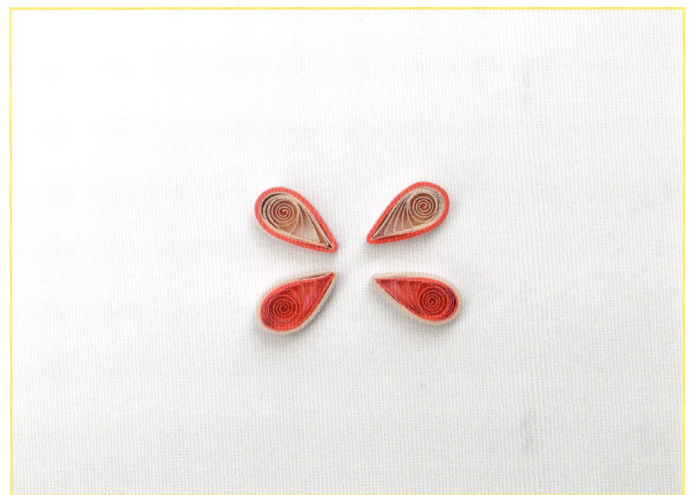

Step 3.

To make the body, make a closed loose coil from a 26 cm length of paper. Make a marquise shape, and press it so it is long and narrow.

Then take a 10 cm strip and fold it in half, making a 'V' shape. Glue the marquise inside the 'V' so it's completely enclosed. The strips at the end can be separated for antennae.

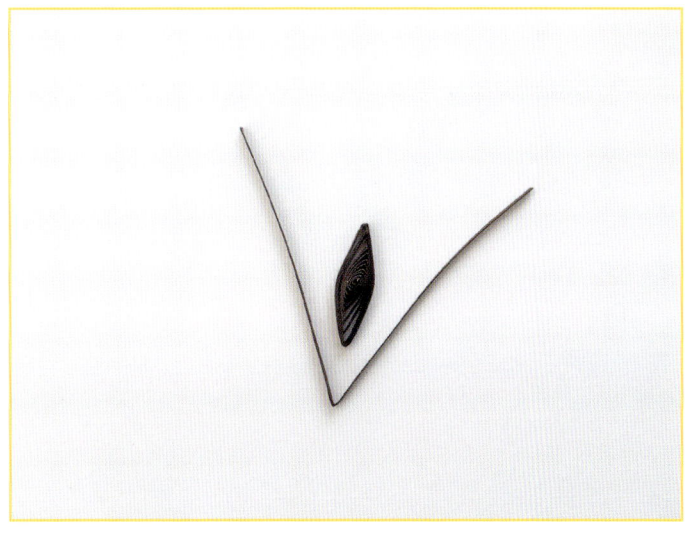

Step 4.

Trim your antennae to the length you want, and give them a gentle curve. If you want to, you can add a curl to the end with your quilling tool.

Step 5.

Glue the body down and arrange the wings on either side. You can add dashed lines to give the impression of a 'dancing' butterfly flying through the air!

The Smaller Butterfly

The smaller butterfly (the size needed for the mandala) is made in exactly the same way, with the following proportions:

Wings: 13 cm strips, wrapped in 13 cm strips.

Body: 19.5 cm strip, wrapped in 10 cm strip.

Project 6.

Sunflower

Sunflowers are such a fabulous sight in summertime, aren't they? Standing so tall and proud, with their faces open to the sunshine.

I remember always having a sunflower growing competition each year, seeing how high they would get.

With this design it is completely up to you how tall your sunflower is. You can always add extra leaves for a longer stem, or make several sunflowers at varying heights.

Step 1.

Take a whole strip (39 cm) of dark brown and make a tight coil.

Take a whole strip of lighter brown and run it through a crimper. (If you have a choice, use a finer crimp.) Glue the end of this crimped strip to the tight coil and gently wrap it around until you get to the end; glue to stop it unravelling.

Glue the flower centre onto your backing card. PLEASE NOTE if you are planning to use the whole design and put your sunflower into a pot, make sure you leave enough space for that and quite a long stem.

Step 2.

Make ten closed loose coils from 19.5 cm strips of paper in yellow and shape them into teardrops. Glue these into place around the centre of the flower, with the points facing outwards.

Arrange the petals so that at the bottom there is a space for the stem to fit between two petals.

Step 3.

Next make another ten closed loose coils from 19.5 cm strips of paper, this time shaping them into marquises. Glue these into place on top of and in between the teardrops below, as shown.

Step 4.

For the flower pot, glue three whole strips of 5 mm width papers end to end to make one long strip.

Wrap it around a border maker or something cylindrical, to make a ring around 2 cm in diameter (this is the 4th step on mine). The only glue you need is a dab right at the beginning and then another dab of glue right at the end to stop it unravelling.

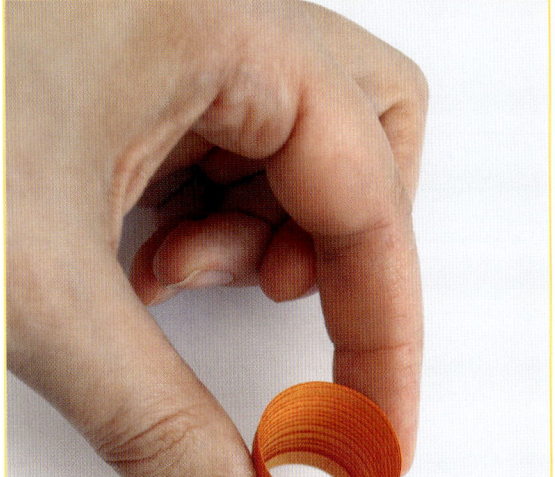

Step 5.

Very slowly and gently, push the middle of the ring of papers out, taking care that the layers stay quite even. If you go too far then the coil will unravel! Ease out the layers so you have a tube of around 2.5 cm in height.

Step 6.

Then we squash the tube into an ellipse shape. This means that we can glue the flower pot down onto the card, but there is still a gap for the stem within it.

Step 7.

Make the stem by taking a 19.5 cm length strip and folding in half end to end. From the fold, add a line of glue and press together and allow to dry. This gives us a stronger stem with a bit more colour.

Put some glue at the tip of one end and insert in between the bottom two petals.

Slide the flower pot into place so the stem is in the pot – and make sure it's not coming out of the bottom! Trim the stem if necessary. When you are happy with the positioning, apply a generous amount of glue to the back of the pot, slide over the stem and gently press into position until it sticks.

There's no need to glue the whole length of the stem to the backing paper, as it will be held in place at the top and in the plant pot. If you wish to secure it further, however, you could add just a little dab of glue where the stem meets the flower pot to hold it extra securely and avoid any movement.

Step 8.

To make the leaves, take whole strips and make closed loose coils. Shape into marquises and then bend so they have a wavy shape. Depending on the height of your sunflower you may want two or four leaves. Glue into place in pairs.

Ice Cream Sundae

An ice cream sundae means both summer sun and celebration to me. There is no better indulgent treat than scoops of your favourite flavours, decorated with hundreds and thousands and of course a flake!

Again you can choose any and all of your favourite colours for this one, and it would make a great design to gift for a special birthday or other celebration.

Step 1.

Using the template provided on page 130 or 131, decide if you want to add any colour to the ice cream or bowl. In my example I have used the template in black to cut out coloured paper shapes for the ice cream and I have chosen a pale yellow for vanilla! Other ways to add colour to the background could be paint, coloured pens or pencils, or even collage.

© Sarah Mason

Then using the on-edge technique, cover the lines around the ice cream, the flake and the bowl – missing out the stem of the bowl.

Don't worry about the wavy line between the scoops of ice cream, the coils we use for the sauce will cover those.

Step 2.

For the stem of the bowl, make the following:

- Three marquise shaped coils from 10 cm strips – placed between the on-edge lines at the bottom of the bowl. Add more if you wish!

- D-shaped coil from a 10 cm strip – to place under the bowl.

- D-shaped coil from a 39 cm strip – to place in the stand.

- Wheatear from a 19.5 cm strip (small loops, adjust to fit the gap between the D-shaped coil and the stand of the bowl).

Step 3.

For the ice cream itself, make a selection of tight coils from 10 cm strips for a colourful topping.

For the sauce, make some coils without gluing down the ends; three from 10 cm strips and three from 19.5 cm strips. For each one, unravel a small tail, so the curve matches the lines on the template and the coil becomes the sauce dripping down the ice cream.

Step 4.

Next for the chocolate flake, make around eight pointed wheatears from 10 cm strips. Place these inside your on-edge lines to fill the space.

Step 5.

As a final flourish, make a closed loose coil from a 19.5 cm strip in red, to make a cherry on top. Add a small length of on-edge strip in brown to make the stem.

Dragonfly

Whenever I see a dragonfly I am always in awe of these beautiful insects. That amazing, iridescent pop of colour is just incredible.

They come in all sorts of colours, such as red, yellow, brown and blue, so you can really enjoy playing with colour with this one. I have used six different colours for the body of mine, in turquoise, blue and a little hint of lilac, with a warm grey for the wings. You can use more colours or fewer. It would also look rather lovely with special, gilded edge papers.

You have a template provided (p. 134 or 135), so you could create a whole host of different designs for this one! I have given you the central line down the body, rather than every coil in its place, so you can really have a play with different designs too, using the same template.

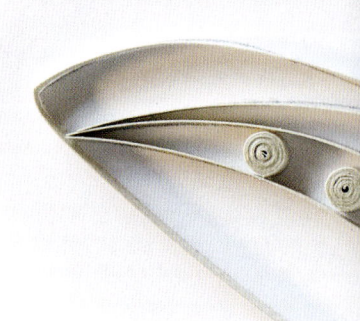

Step 1.

Take a strip of 13 cm length and make a heart-shaped scroll. Place this so the top of the scroll is in line with the top of the wings on your template.

Above, make a teardrop from a strip 19.5 cm long and place this so the rounded end rests on top of the heart scroll.

At the top, make a teardrop from a 5 cm strip and place in the centre at the base of the antennae.

Step 2.

Make a tight coil from a 5 cm strip, and place this inside the heart-shaped scroll.

Make two teardrops from 10 cm strips and place these, with rounded ends together, at the top of the larger teardrop.

Create two tight coils from 5 cm strips to place either side of the small top teardrop.

Step 3.

Make six tight coils from 5 cm strips, to place either side of the large teardrop, three each side.

You can choose any colours you wish for your dragonfly, but bear in mind that it's a good idea for balance to keep them symmetrical.

Place two teardrops, from 10 cm strips, either side of the heart-shaped scroll.

Also from a 10 cm strip, create a closed loose coil, keeping it as a circle, to place underneath.

Step 4.

Make another heart-shaped scroll as before, using a 13 cm strip. Place this so the point is touching the circle above. Either side of that, and another inside, place tight coils made from 5 cm strips.

Step 5.

Using a border maker or something similar, make some open circles of approximately 11 mm in diameter (this is the 2nd step on my border maker). Pinch into a teardrop.

Inside, place a closed loose coil and a tight coil, each made from 10 cm strips.

Either side of the tip place two tight coils made from 5 cm strips, leaving space for the next section of tail.

Step 6.

Repeat the actions from Step 5 until you get to the bottom of the tail, using different shades or colours as you wish, but remembering the symmetry of your design.

Step 7.

To make the antennae, use strips of 3 cm length and roll the whole length. Then unravel the end to match the shape on the template. Glue down.

Cut a strip approximately 13 mm long and curve. This will sit at the top of the head.

Use the on-edge technique for making the legs, following the lines on the template.

Step 8.

Again using the on-edge technique, create the wings following the guidelines on the template.

Step 9.

Optional: if you would like to add more decoration to the wings, you can. I like both the plain wings and decorated. In my example of the decorated wings, I have used wheatears of different sizes and tight coils from 10 cm lengths.

Part 3:

The fanfare of summer is drawing to a close and it's time to prepare for the darker days ahead. The light can still be absolutely glorious this time of year though, and there is so much colour outside in early autumn.

With the leaves on the trees changing colour, crops being harvested and animals preparing themselves for the winter ahead, it's such a beautiful but sometimes bittersweet season. A plentiful harvest is something to celebrate, but much work to be done!

Autumn colours become slightly deeper now with tones of red and gold to reflect the leaves changing colour, ripening fruits and harvested crops.

Project 9.

Falling Leaves

There is nothing else out there like scuffing through fallen leaves on a bright, sunny autumn day! That gorgeous crunchy sound at each step, kicking the leaves in the air to watch them fall again.

The colours are a riot of deep greens, reds and golds, and in this project you can mix up those shades from leaf to leaf, or even combine in the same leaf to make a patchwork of autumn hues.

Similar to the butterflies in Project 5, these leaf designs can be used separately for cards and gift tags, or combined together to make a larger design. To give you added inspiration, I have taken the leaves and added them to the word 'AUTUMN' to make a complete design, and have provided this template for you too (p. 132 or 133).

Leaf 1

Cut a length of paper and fold in half, end to end, to make a 'V' shape. Apply glue to the sides of the top half of your leaf and insert into the point of the V. Then apply glue to the bottom half and the rest of the strip below. Secure together, so the leaf is sandwiched between the two sides, and the remaining strip forms the stem.

Step 3.

Make a selection of leaves in a variety of autumn shades!

Step 1.

Use a full strip (39 cm) and make a closed loose coil. Shape into a half circle. Make a second. Glue together along the straight edges.

Step 2.

Take a length of paper strip and glue one end near the point of your glued-together leaf shapes. Wrap twice around the shapes to help bind them together. Cut off any excess and glue the end down.

Leaf 2

Step 1.

Make the following:

- Three closed loose coils using 19.5 cm length strips, shaped into marquises.

- Two closed loose coils using 13 cm length strips, also shaped into marquises.

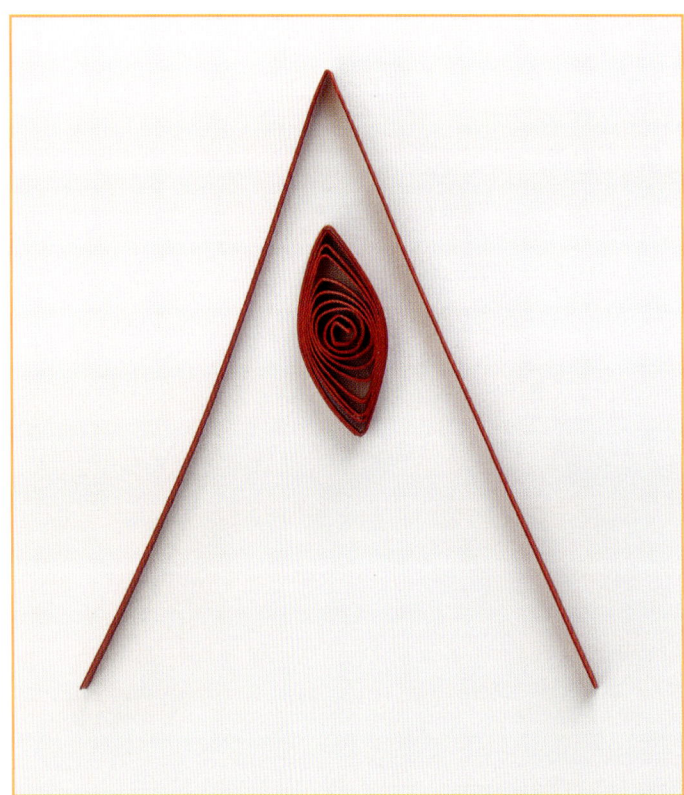

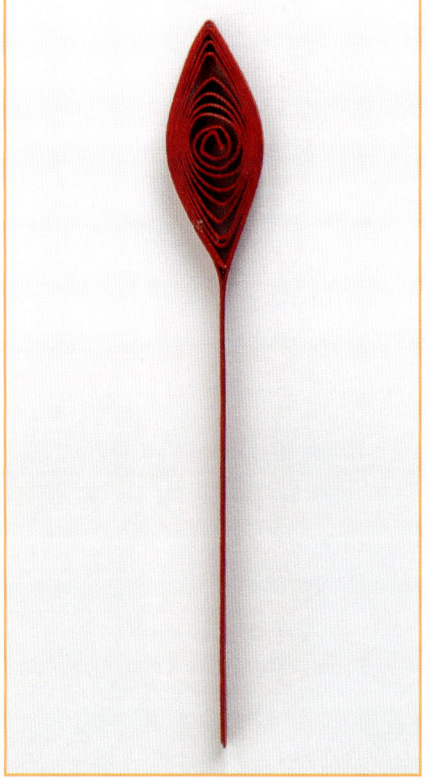

Step 2.

Take a length of paper and fold in half to make a 'V' shape. Glue one of your larger marquises into the fold of the V, and seal it all the way to the end of the strip.

Step 3.

Glue the two remaining larger marquises either side of the first, and then the smaller two either side of those.

Step 4.

Make a selection of these leaves using a variety of autumnal colours.

Leaf 3

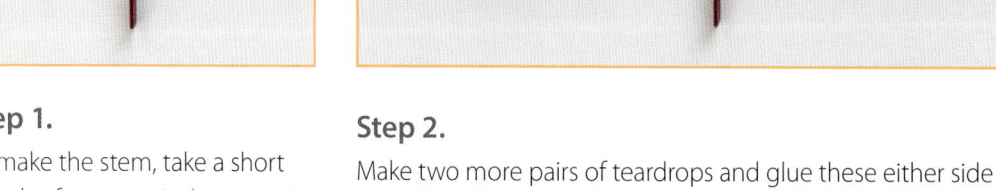

Step 1.

To make the stem, take a short length of paper strip (approx. 11 cm) and fold in half end to end. Starting at the fold, apply glue to the whole length and press closed – so you're doubling the strength of the strip.

Use 19.5 cm strips to make two closed loose coils, shaped into teardrops.

Glue these at one end, either side of your stem as shown.

Step 2.

Make two more pairs of teardrops and glue these either side of the first.

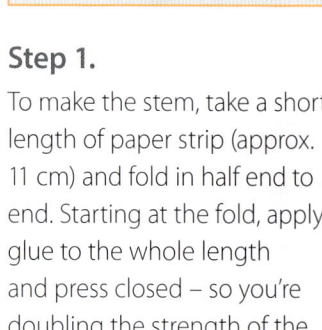

Step 3.

Make a number of these leaves in a selection of autumnal colours.

Leaf 4

Step 1.

Make nine closed loose coils from 10 cm strips, shaped into marquises.

As we did with leaf 2, fold a strip in half and glue one of the marquises into the 'V' shape, and glue the rest of the stem together.

Step 2.

Glue the rest of the marquises down the stem on either side.

Step 3.

Make a number of these leaves in a selection of autumnal colours.

Leaf 5

Step 1.

Using 19.5 cm strips of paper make five closed loose coils. Pinch them into marquise shapes first and then curve each pointed end in opposite directions using your fingers to give an S-shaped coil.

Take one of the S shapes and repeat the technique for leaves 2 and 4, using a folded strip and gluing inside to create the stem.

Step 2.

Arrange the other four S-shaped coils either side on the stem and glue in place.

Step 3.

Make a number of these leaves in a selection of autumnal colours.

WHAT'S NEXT?

These leaves can be used on their own for cards and gift tags, or combined to create a framed picture, such as the word art design provided.

To make this, simply cut out the letters in coloured paper or card and then edge them in a matching coloured strip of paper.

Then arrange the leaves around the letters at random. Play with their positioning until you are happy you have a balanced composition, and then glue in place.

Project 10.

Hedgehog

I am so lucky where I live to have an active population of this endangered species, and have hedgehogs visit our garden every night. I have a wildlife camera so I get to watch their antics! Ever since I read *The Tale of Mrs Tiggy-Winkle* as a child, I have been charmed by these distinctive creatures.

With the nights getting longer in the autumn hedgehogs are very active, as they prepare for hibernation, and they appear a bit earlier in the day. You are therefore more likely to see them in this season than in any other.

A hedgehog is a surprisingly hard animal to portray in quilling as it has such a distinct look. All those spines, which are actually multiple shades of brown, are particularly tricky. So for this cute and quirky hedgehog I have used a paper crimper to add to that impression of multiple spikes. The added benefit of this is that the crimped paper is easier to glue on its edge, giving added stability.

For this project you will find it easiest to glue it down directly onto some backing card. This would be a good one to use your fringing scissors to cut out, if you wished. Then it would make a great magnet, or you could glue it to a wooden peg to use as a note holder. You could also create a larger scene to place your hedgehog in a garden or woodland.

Step 1.

Using a border maker and two strips of paper glued end to end, make a circle approximately 42 mm in diameter – for me this is step 8 on the round border maker. However, this is a design that you can easily adapt for different sizes.

Apply the glue to the edge on one side of your circle. As you place it down on your paper, gently squeeze it to make it an oval, as shown.

Step 2.

Make a selection of S scrolls using both 19.5 cm and 10 cm length strips. These are your 'fillers' so start to place them inside the body of the hedgehog. Begin gluing these into place, starting at the edge.

Step 3.

Fill the whole of the hedgehog with S scrolls. Don't worry about leaving a few gaps, but if you have a large hole you can always use a small single coil to fill in.

Step 4.

Using strips 19.5 cm long, make four closed loose coils. Shape into teardrops – two for the feet, and two for the arms. Use your thumb to shape them a little to match the curve of the body and glue into place.

Step 5.

Take a 10 cm strip of paper in a light pink for the inside of the ear. Make a closed loose coil.

Using another 10 cm strip in the same colour as the body, glue this to the pink coil and wrap it around, gluing the end down so it won't unravel. Then shape into a D-shape coil, adding a little curve so it sits well on the curve of the head.

Repeat this step to create the other ear.

Have a play with positioning the ears, and when you are happy, glue them down.

Step 6.

Before I start to place any spines on my hedgehog, I like to draw a guideline of where the spines will go up to.

To do this, I take a strip of paper, tucking the end into the corner by the foot. Then I take it around the top of the body and cut it to a length that creates a nice loop around the hedgehog, and tuck the other end in. I then use this shape to draw around, very lightly in pencil.

Step 7.

For the spines, I use two shades of brown – a darker one and a lighter one. Put a single strip of each through a crimper. If you have a choice, it's also nice to use the finer and larger wheels on the crimper for different effects.

For the first colour, measure a length from the side of the hedgehog to just past your drawn line. Cut the length you need and glue into place.

Step 8.

In this way, put a few spines on one side and then a few on the other. Keep working your way around, leaving gaps in between spines.

Step 9.

Keep working in this way all the way around the body. Don't worry about any gaps or uneven parts, as this can be remedied by simply adding more strips, and if needed a different length of strip.

Step 10.

Next work your way around again with a different shade, sliding your strips into the gaps. Keep going this way until you are happy with your hedgehog.

Step 11.

Make a tight coil from a length of 19.5 cm for the nose. Play around with positioning the nose and googly eyes (or if you prefer you can make eyes from paper) and when you are happy, glue these in place.

Project 11.

Toadstool

With hundreds of varieties of fungi out there in our woodlands, this classic style of toadstool, based on the fly agaric variety, is so distinctive and fun to portray. They are often associated with fairies, gnomes and other mythical creatures of the woodland – so maybe that's an idea you'd like to incorporate with your design? A simpler idea would be to repeat this design in other colours to create a collection, or add eyes to make toadstool creatures!

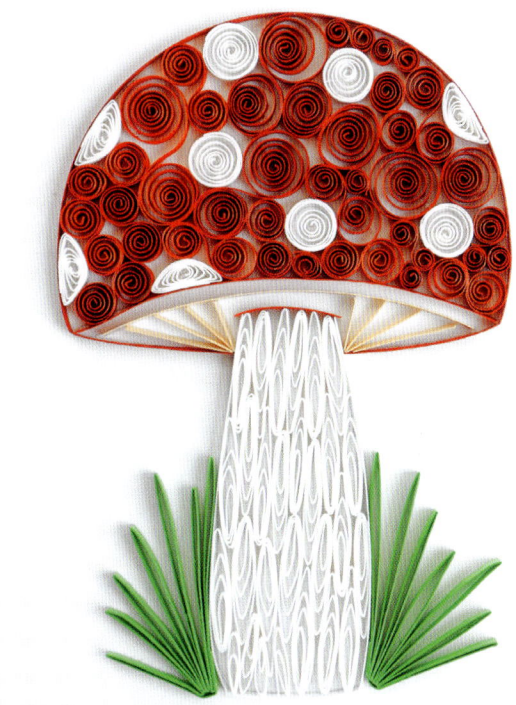

© Sarah Mason

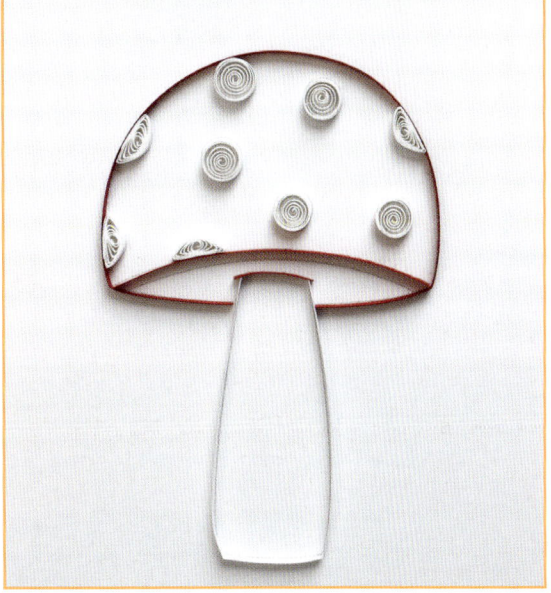

Step 1.

Using the template, outline the top of the toadstool with the on-edge technique in red, and the stalk of the toadstool in white, as shown.

Step 2.

Make nine closed loose coils with 10 cm strips in white. Shape four of them into half circles to fit against the outside edges of the toadstool top. Glue over the relevant shapes on the template.

Step 3.

Make a selection of S scrolls using mostly 10 cm strips. You may wish to have one variant of red, or use different shades for added depth. I have used 13 in mine, in two similar shades of red, and four or five from 19.5 cm strips; you may need a couple more or less. Fit these in and around your glued-down spots to fill the space. Don't worry about small gaps, but if a gap is very noticeable you can make a very small coil to fill the space.

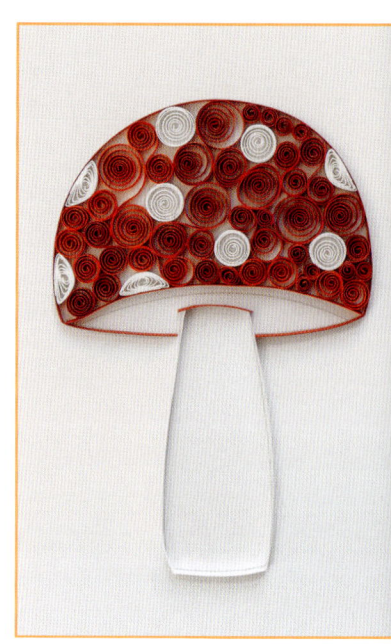

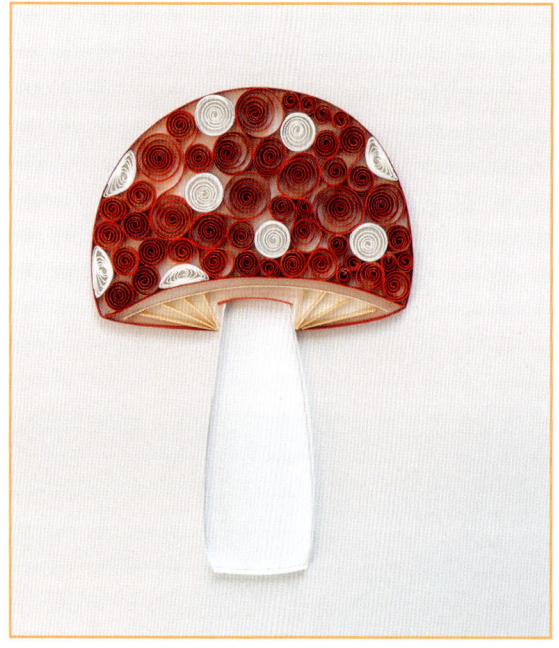

Step 4.

In the area under the cap of the toadstool, add some on-edge papers on the line given, plus add three or four diagonal lines radiating out from the centre, as shown.

Step 5.

Using 10 cm strips make a selection of pointed wheatears. (I used approximately 28 in mine.) Starting from the top of the stem, glue these down side by side.

Step 6.

Fill in the whole of the stem this way. When you get to the bottom you may need to make some very short wheatears with just a loop or two to fill in any gaps.

Step 7.

Take a whole strip of paper (39 cm), and starting at one end fold the paper in a concertina style as shown. Make your first fold around 3 cm long, and make each fold after that slightly shorter than the one before. Aim for around seven folds.

Step 8.

Pinch the folds so the paper meets at the base. Trim any excess paper off, leaving just a small amount to fold around the base and glue down. Then fan out the individual pieces of grass.

Repeat this process so you have two tufts of grass.

Step 9.

Place the tufts of grass on either side of your toadstool and glue in place.

Pumpkin

While we often see pumpkins carved and lit up as Halloween lanterns, this humble fruit is also quite beautiful in form and colour. I have emphasised this with this design, celebrating the form and segments of the pumpkin.

At its heart it is a really simple repeating design, but if you play with the colours then you get this wonderful, detailed effect. I have cut out each segment by tracing on paper using the template with black lines (p. 138), using a different shade of orange for each one.

Then on top of those, the coils are also a mixture of oranges, one shade in each segment. So one full flower motif may have a segment dividing line going through it, making that individual flower two shades. Other flowers wholly in one segment will be all in one colour.

A simple design made more complex by combining with colour mixes.

Step 1.

On your printed template for this design you can add colour to the sections of the pumpkin with paint or pens, or use the version with black lines to cut out coloured paper for each section, as I have done in this example. I have chosen six different shades of orange, and used Tant paper squares.

You can see on mine there are a few slight gaps between the cut out shapes, but that's fine as they will get covered with the quilling. I use a glue stick for these, as a wetter glue can cause paper to ripple.

Step 2.

Use the on-edge technique to outline the whole of the pumpkin and each segment. I have used one mid-orange paper to do the whole pumpkin, and a green for the stalk.

Step 3.

For the flower decorations on my pumpkin I have colour matched my paper strips to my background as closely as I can.

Make a selection of closed loose coils shaped into marquises, using both 13 cm strips and 10 cm strips.

Place your flowers evenly throughout the pumpkin on the segment lines. There are six petals per flower, so apart from the part-flowers on the outer edges, you will need three of one colour for one section and three in the colour of the adjoining section.

Step 4.

Make a selection of open coils in different sizes and shades. (This is a really good way of using up any offcuts and odd lengths of paper you have around!) For something this size, a maximum length of 10 cm will probably be as big as you need to go. You can really go to town with the number of open coils if you want to, or be more sparing with them.

For this part, I like to mix up the different shades, using all the colours across all sections.

Step 5.

Finish off your pumpkin by adding some on-edge lines into the stalk.

Part 4: *Winter*

Winter, a time to curl up and get cosy with our loved ones, to decorate our houses and mark the end of one year, and the start of another.

Making the most of the coldest days of the year can cheer up the long nights and bring brightness to the dark. Wrapping up warmly and enjoying a snowy landscape can be a special experience, and admiring the plants and animals that thrive in this environment can lift the spirits.

It might be easy to think that colours in the winter can be dark and dismal, but look again! They may be softer and darker in general, but there are also pops of colour. At a time of celebration for many, the joyful nature of coloured lights in the dark is a symbol that all things pass, and winter does not last forever.

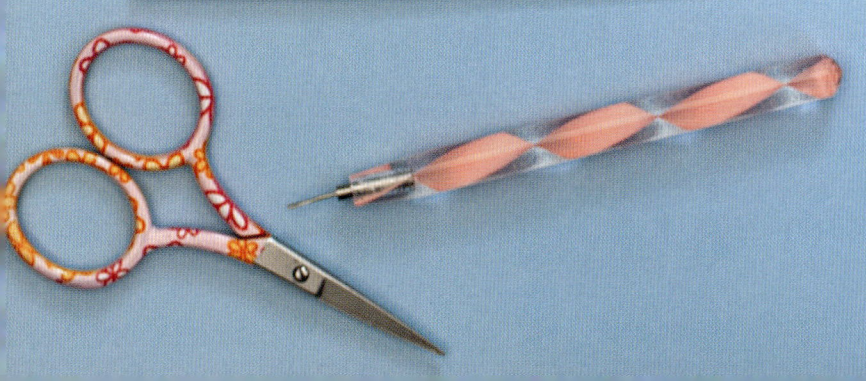

Project 13.

Poinsettia

These beautiful plants, with their showy red leaves-that-aren't petals, are fabulous to have in the house and brighten up the darker days of winter. But if, like me, you don't have green fingers and struggle to keep them alive, this is the perfect alternative!

A real plant adds glorious colour to a dark winter day and this quilled version can too. You can make them in regular quilling paper, or to make them extra festive you can use gilded edge paper, or added glitter to help catch the light.

These are wonderful for gift tags and toppers, Christmas cards, and my favourite – hanging decorations for your Christmas tree.

They use just two types of coils, layered up: tight coils for the centre and elongated 'D' shaped coils.

Step 1.

Using 44 cm strips, make ten elongated D-shaped coils in green.

Glue them together in pairs along their straight edges.

Glue the green leaves down to your backing card, arranging the leaves evenly. There will be a hole in the middle of the arrangement; this is fine as it will be hidden later.

If you would like to make these as hanging decorations, you can glue them down onto backing card and cut out your finished plant. Alternatively, you can glue the leaves to each other, rather than onto a surface, so your finished creation will also show the light through the leaves.

Step 2.

Repeat Step 1 to make the same shapes in red, using the following lengths, and gluing into pairs to make the leaves:

   10 x 44 cm lengths

   10 x 22 cm lengths

Then glue the large red leaves on top, in between the green leaves.

Step 3.

Glue the next layer of smaller red leaves, again placing in between the leaves below.

Step 4.

Make seven tight coils from 11 cm strips of yellow.

Arrange them so there is one in the centre, and glue the others around it.

Place this in the centre of the poinsettia to complete your design.

Snowflakes

The most recognisable symbol of winter weather, many of us are taught to be fascinated by snowflakes from a very early age. I remember well many a craft session folding and cutting paper circles to make a never-ending selection of designs.

And nowadays I love to quill a snowflake or two. It is popularly believed that each and every snowflake is unique in shape and style, and with all the quilling shapes at our disposal, we can never run out of shapes and styles to imagine!

Here I share two designs to get you started. As your confidence grows I am sure you will start to have ideas about mixing and matching different techniques to create an abundance of different designs.

Once again, these are wonderful for gift tags, toppers and Christmas cards, as well as hanging decorations. Using white or silver paper with a coloured background can really make your designs pop, too.

I often like to use a specialist gilded edge quilling paper for my snowflakes. The gilded edge gives a lovely shine to the quilling, and as it is only on one side, you can reverse some of your coils as I have with this one, to have a two-sided decoration. Of course, you can use any kind of colour or type of paper for your snowflakes, and they can be used for a multitude of purposes.

When you make your snowflake, you can either glue it straight down onto the surface you are using, or simply glue the coils to each other as you go along, so then you can place it into your design at a later stage, or make it into a hanging decoration.

Unless specified, all the elements for these snowflakes are using 11 cm strips of paper.

Snowflake 1

Step 1.

Make a tight coil for the very centre of your snowflake, followed by six more to arrange around the outside, in your chosen colours. Glue in place.

Step 2.

Make six more tight coils and glue them in place in the next row, so each one sits between two on the previous row.

Step 3.

Make two closed loose coils and pinch into marquise shapes. Glue together at the point.

Then take a strip and fold in half end to end. Starting at the fold, put a line of glue all the way along and press together. This gives you a strip with extra strength for the 'branch' of the snowflake. Cut a length approximately 1.5 cm. Put a dab of glue at the end and wedge this between the two marquise shapes.

Step 4.

Glue your branch in between two of the outer tight coils as shown.

Step 5.

Make two more closed loose coils, pinch into marquise shapes and glue these to the end of your branch.

Make a tight coil and nestle this in between the two marquises.

Step 6.

You've made one branch of your snowflake. Repeat this five more times to complete your snowflake.

Snowflake 2

Step 1.
Make six closed loose coils and pinch to marquise shapes. Glue together point to point to create a flower/star shape as shown.

Step 2.
Make a heart-shaped scroll, leaving approximately 5 mm between the point and the bottom of each coil, and glue into place between two 'petals'. Don't glue the coiled ends together yet, as the branch of the snowflake will be inserted and glued between them.

Then take a length of paper and fold in half end to end. Starting at the fold, put a line of glue all the way along and press together. This gives you a strip with extra strength for the 'branch' of the snowflake. Cut a length approximately 2 cm. Put a dab of glue on one end, and also where the heart-shaped scrolls meet the branch to secure it in place.

Step 3.
Make two closed loose coils, shaped into marquises, and glue at the end of the branch.

Step 4.

Use a strip of 22 cm length and wrap it around the handle of your quilling tool, the smallest step on your border maker or something similar, to create a border that is approximately 1 cm in diameter (outside edge). Just use a dab of glue at the beginning, where the paper joins, and a dab of glue at the end to secure it. Pinch it into a teardrop. Glue into place, nestled between the two marquises.

Make a tight coil and glue this into place inside the teardrop.

Step 5.

You've made one branch of your snowflake. Repeat this five more times to complete your snowflake.

Project 15.

Penguin

Whenever I think of a snowy, wintry landscape, this is one animal that would be at the forefront of my mind. By now you may have noticed that I like to create cute, quirky animals with googly eyes to brighten someone's day. These comical creatures really lend themselves to this kind of design.

Like the hedgehog and rabbit, these penguins can vary each time you make them, giving them added character and charm. Cut out and added to a wooden peg, you have a lovely note holder, or they make wonderful Christmas cards. You can further personalise them by adding different accessories.

Step 1.

Take two strips of quilling paper (39 cm) and glue them together end to end so you have one long strip. Wrap it around the largest step of the border maker to make a circle.

Apply the glue to one side of the circle, and as you place it onto your backing card, shape it with your fingers so it is more penguin-shaped – narrower at the top and wider at the bottom.

Step 2.

Take a full length strip of white and roll into a closed loose coil. Then shape it into a soft triangle and glue in place in the centre at the bottom of the penguin.

Step 3.

a. Make a selection of S scrolls using both 19.5 cm and 10 cm length strips. Start to place these into

the remaining space in the body of the penguin. These are simply a filler to give colour and texture, so you can squash them together if needed, and if there are any gaps, you can fill with a small single coil.

b. Fill the whole penguin.

Step 4.

To make the wings, take a whole strip of paper and make a closed loose coil. Shape into a half circle and then curve around your thumb a little more so the wing will follow the shape of the body a little. Repeat this for the other wing.

For the feet, again use a whole strip of paper and make two tight coils (one for each foot). Before gluing the end down, release the pressure a little so you just start to get a hole appear in the centre. Then secure the end before shaping into an oval.

Glue the wings and feet into place as shown.

Step 5.

Use a 19.5 cm strip of orange for the beak. In the same way as the feet, make a tight coil, then release the pressure giving you a small hole in the centre before gluing down the end. Then shape into a triangle.

Use googly eyes and glue them all down onto your penguin.

Variations

This is the kind of simple make that you can have a lot of fun with, as we're not following an exact pattern. Each one will be slightly different and by changing the features they can have different characters.

You could try smaller feet and wings, a bigger beak, moving the eyes – even adding accessories. Have a play with personalising your penguins!

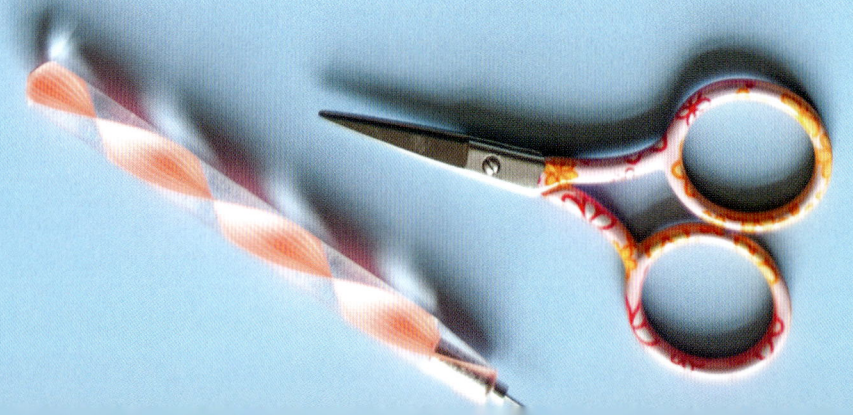

Ice Skate

The perfect way to enjoy the freezing cold weather, ice skating is a wonderful winter treat with more and more ice rinks popping up in towns and cities each festive season now.

While I've never owned a beautiful pair of ice skates myself, I love the silhouette of these boots so much I decided to design my own dream pair instead! With a white background, I have used a mix of soft pastel colours and slightly bolder teal and grey to give the impression of frost and ice.

With the template provided (p. 140 or 141), you are given guidelines for all the elements I have used, but if you wanted to have a coloured background and create your own design, that's another route you can enjoy.

Step 1.

Print out your template onto good quality paper or card.

For the blade, you can either colour it in using a light grey paint or marker pen, or as I have done in the example here, use the separate template to cut out coloured paper to fill the shape. If you're using coloured paper, I recommend a glue stick to fix it to your design, as it's less wet and won't affect the paper.

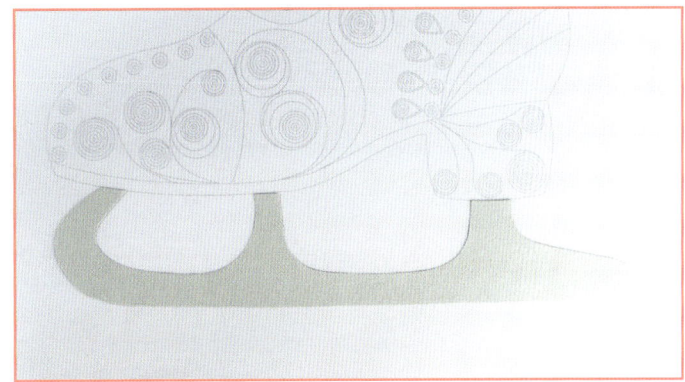

Step 2.

Using the on-edge technique start to edge the blade of the skate. Here I have used a very close colour match to the paper. Continue edging the boot in white.

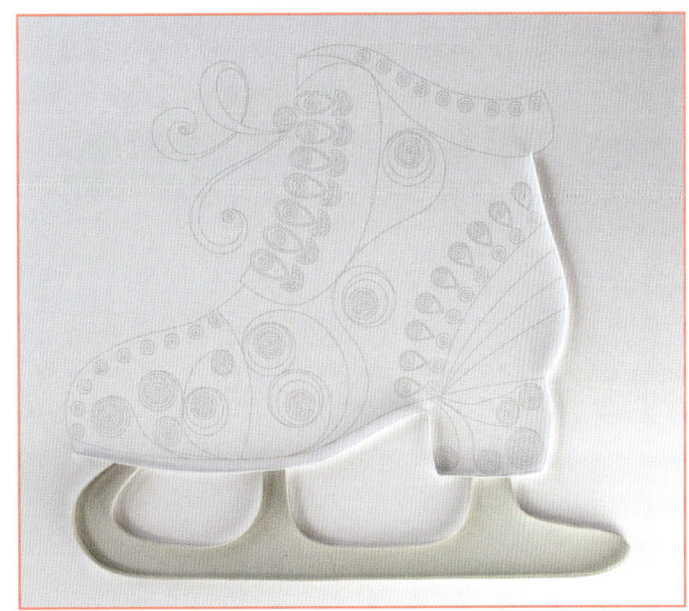

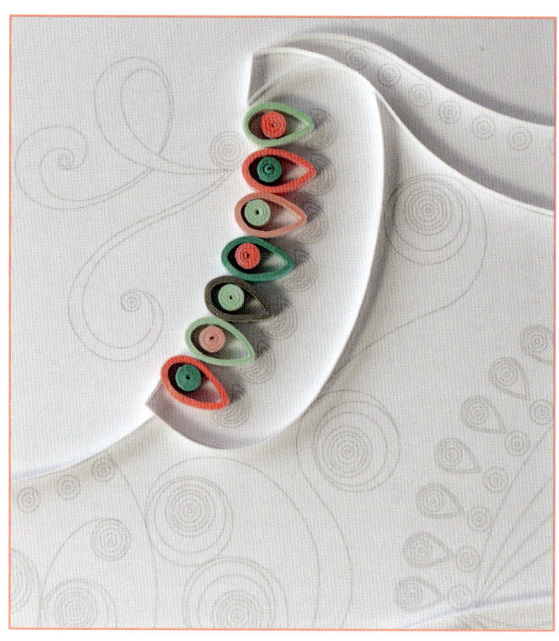

Step 3.

Work your way around the outside of the ice skate, edging it as shown.

Step 4.

For the eyelets:

Using a 19.5 cm strip of paper in your chosen colour, wrap it around the handle of your quilling tool, the smallest step on your border maker, or a pencil or something similar, to create a border that is approximately 8 mm in diameter. Just use a dab of glue at the beginning, where the paper joins, and a dab of glue at the end to secure it.

When you have your circle, pinch it into a teardrop and place onto the template as shown.

Then using a 10 cm strip of paper, make a tight coil to go inside it. Repeat this six times, so you have seven in total.

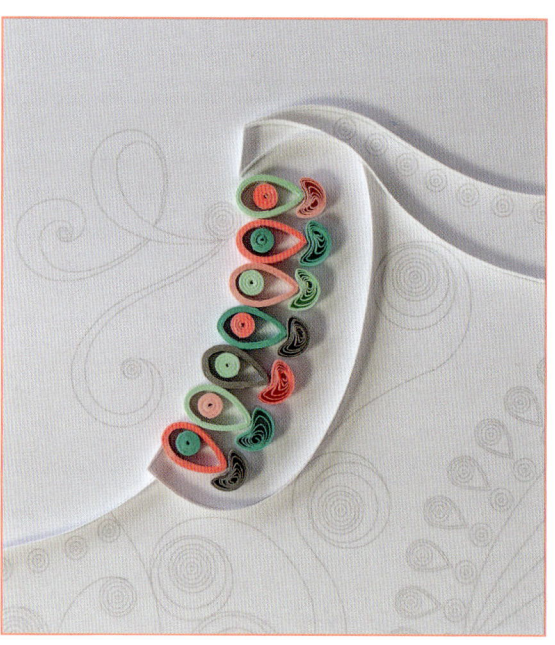

Step 5.

Use a 10 cm strip of paper and make a 7 mm closed loose coil. Make into a banana shape and place at the pointed end of the eyelet hole. Repeat six more times so there is one on each eyelet.

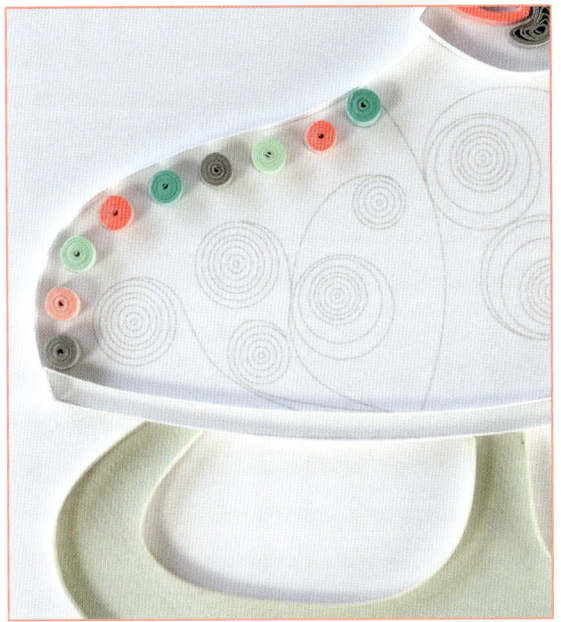

Step 6.

Using strips of paper 10 cm long, make nine tight coils. Place these on your template in the toe of the skate.

Step 7.

Make the open coils (as shown on page 22) for the toe of the skate. For the three larger open coils, use 19.5 cm strips as your starting point, and for the smaller two, use 10 cm strips.

Step 8.

Next to the heel; cut lengths of strips to cover the single lines and glue in place.

Step 9.

Using strips of 10 cm length, make nine tight coils and nine closed loose coils pinched into teardrop shapes. Glue into place on the template as shown.

Step 10.

Using 19.5 cm strips, make four two-colour open coils using two contrasting colours of your choice. Place on the template where indicated.

Step 11.

For the heel: for the larger open coil use a 19.5 cm strip; for the four smaller open coils use 10 cm strips. Glue in place on your template.

Step 12.

For the laces: the knot is a closed loose coil made with a 10 cm strip of paper. For the bow, use the on-edge technique. You will find it easier to start at the end of the laces, and curl a small section first. This makes it easier to glue down to get you

started, and then for the second strip of paper, somewhere to tuck it into. Curl the paper with your fingers/blunt edge of your scissors so you have roughly the shape you want before gluing down.

Step 13.

And lastly, add three on-edge straight lines onto the blade, in a lighter colour than you've used to fill it, to suggest the glint of metal!

Part 5:

Four Seasons Mandala

I recently went on a workshop to learn to create drawn mandalas, and I was blown away by this beautiful practice.

The word mandala comes from the Sanskrit word for 'circle'. And when you look in the natural world, the examples of circles within circles making up every living thing are quite astounding. A mandala is often used in prayer and meditation in Asian cultures, representing different elements of the universe. Bringing quilling and mandalas together feels like a harmonious match and I hope you feel the calming benefits while you create your design.

To have one design that can represent all four of our seasons in motion, it seemed a good idea to wrap up our time together and our journey through the seasons by also bringing together all your quilling skills – in this one beautiful mandala design.

Rather than map out every single coil on the template, as this is quite a detailed design, I have instead provided you with a regular mandala grid, so it's suitable for this design as well as any others you wish to create in the future.

As with all the other templates, I have provided you with two versions, in light grey and black lines (p. 142 and 143).

You will get the best results for this one if you use the template with dark lines and use a lightbox. In these instructions, I have shown myself making the mandala by quilling onto a printed version of the light grey lines. This just means that some lines will still show through.

If you opt for this way of making your mandala, and the lines bother you, perhaps you can come up with an imaginative idea to disguise the lines? Tiny gemstones perhaps, or tiny tight coils?

The circle is divided up into 12 equal segments, with three – or a quarter of the circle – for each season.

I have used four different shades each of yellow, green and blue to represent the changing of each season as we go around the circle, and the sun, land and sky. For instance, I have chosen a very pale yellow to represent a weak, winter sun, but a darker green and a duskier shade of blue. In the summer, I've chosen bright and bold colours. For spring I have pastel shades, and for autumn some rich tones – all representing the changing light and foliage.

It can be easy to get mixed up with which shade goes where, so to make it a bit easier for yourself, keep your mandala grid the same way up at the start of each step. I have photographed it with spring as the top left quarter, then moving clockwise through the seasons; so summer in the top right, autumn bottom right, and winter in the bottom left.

Step 1.

You may wish to create your mandala keeping a white background. Here you will see that I have cut out the circle to start with, and glued this down onto my backing card. If you are using the dark lines with the lightbox, you might find it easier to lightly tack your circle with strips of masking tape to your template, and add it to a coloured background at the end of the project.

Once you have done that, we will start with the sun at the centre.

Take a full strip (39 cm) of each of the four shades of yellow, and join end to end. Coil up into one big tight coil. (You might find it easier to take it off the quilling tool after a while and roll it between your fingers.) Glue this down right in the centre of your mandala grid.

On your grid, imagine that it is the face of a clock, so the line at the top is 12, followed by 1 o'clock, 2 o'clock moving around the clockface.

Using 10 cm strips make three tight coils in each shade of yellow and we will place them as follows:

- Add your colours for summer at lines 1 o'clock and 2 o'clock.

- At 3 o'clock, use your spring yellow.

- At 4 and 5 o'clock, use your autumn yellows.

- At 6 o'clock you will place one summer shade of yellow.

- At 7 and 8 o'clock, it is winter.

- At 9 o'clock use your autumn coil.

- At 10 and 11 o'clock you need your spring colours.

- And finally at 12 o'clock another winter coil.

- Glue down.

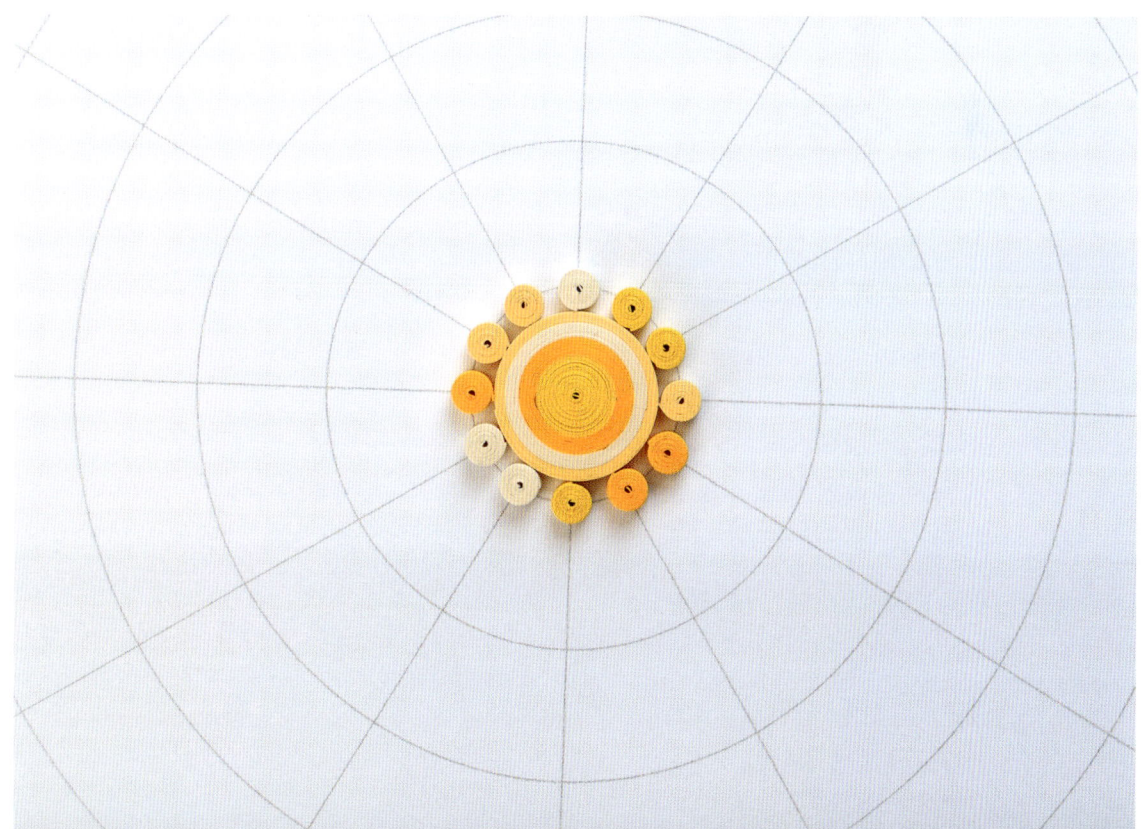

Step 2.

Make three closed loose coils from 19.5 cm strips (11 mm circles) in each shade of yellow (12 in total). Shape them into marquises, and squeeze so they are quite narrow.

Place these in the corresponding quarter of the circle so one tip is in between the tight coils, and the other tip is central in its own segment.

Step 3.

From this step onwards, all strips should be 10 cm unless otherwise stated. Use three closed loose coils (7 mm circles) in each shade of yellow (12 in total). Shape into marquises.

Place these above each corresponding tight coil in the same colour, so two within its seasonal quarter, plus one other between seasons.

Step 4.

In the blues, make two heart-shaped scrolls using each of the four shades you have selected for the four seasons.

On the mandala template, these are placed over the two small marquises in each season, with the points of the hearts on the segment lines.

Step 5.

Make three wheatears in each shade of blue (12 in total).

Glue these down in their seasons so there is one central wheatear in the middle between the heart-shaped scrolls, and one each side with the points on the corners of that segment.

Step 6.

Make four wheatears in each shade of green (16 in total).

Place these with the tip of the wheatear pointing towards the centre of the circle so they slide neatly between the blue wheatears.

Step 7.

Make one open coil in each shade of blue. Place these on the right as you move clockwise through each spread of wheatears, so the coil sits on the small marquise.

Step 8.

Make another open coil in each shade of blue, and moving anti-clockwise, these coils sit on top of the previous ones.

Step 9.

Make two S scrolls in each shade of green (eight in total).

Glue these in place on the line in between the fan of wheatears and the open coils, in their relevant season.

Step 10.

Make the seasonal elements as follows:

Spring – make the smaller version of the celandine from Spring, pages 30–33.

Summer – make the smaller version of the butterfly from Summer, pages 50–52.

Autumn – make leaf number 2 from Autumn, pages 70–71.

Winter – make a star as follows:

To make the star, print out the template and place under some coloured paper OR cut it out and trace around it lightly. Cut five lengths of 2 cm and fold in half. Glue these down on each point of the star to edge it. Then cut around the shape.

Place each of these elements above the relevant wheatear fan, centrally so the top of the emblem just crosses the penultimate line before the edge of the mandala.

If you want to, place the added coils on the star, using strips 5 cm long, folding in half and coiling outwards.

Step 11.

Make one closed loose coil in each shade of blue, and shape into a teardrop. Glue this down on the outside edge above the corresponding element pointing into the centre of the mandala.

Make two S scrolls in each shade of green, and two tight coils in each shade of blue.

With the teardrop in the middle, place the S scrolls either side, and the tight coils on the outside of those in each section.

Step 12.

Make two open coils from each of the blues and the greens. Make a gently curving tail of around 4 cm. (Measure one with a ruler and then measure the others against that first one.)

Place the greens either side of the outer teardrop so the coil sits on the very outside edge of the mandala grid.

The blues also go either side of the teardrop, and the coils will sit on the second grid line in from the outside, not quite reaching the centre in that segment.

Step 13.

To make sure you can clearly see each step that we follow, the steps from now on will demonstrate what to do concentrating on the spring and summer segments. Whatever we do for spring, however, you will then need to repeat for all the seasons. Take your time and pay close attention to the relevant colours changing for each season. I recommend repeating each step for all seasons before moving on to the next one, rather than completing one season at a time.

It is good practice to make the elements for each step, place them on your design and check you are happy before gluing anything down.

If you like to make all the elements in advance, keep lots of containers with all your seasonal colours separated (recycled yoghurt pots can come in very handy for this).

Make two wheatears in each shade of green, blue and yellow.

Starting at the outer edge, insert a green (tip pointing inwards) and then a yellow wheatear (tip pointing outwards) between the S scroll and the tail of the green open coil on each side.

Then add the blue wheatear (tip pointing inwards) between the two tails of the green and blue open coils.

Step 14.

Make four teardrops in each shade of green and two in each shade of blue.

Also make two smaller teardrops from 5 cm strips in each shade of green.

Place these along the tails of the open coils to decorate them, as shown.

Step 15.

Next we're going to be working on the section line between each of the seasons, so the colours will be one season on one side, and another on the other side.

You need two heart-shaped scrolls in each shade of blue. Place these point to point, using the grid lines to guide you, on the third cross from the outside of the circle.

Then make two open coils in each shade of green from 5 cm length strips of paper. These go on the outer side of the heart-shaped scrolls, to form another heart shape across two seasons.

Step 16.

Make two S scrolls in each shade of blue. Use these to join the heart-shaped scrolls in the same colour, to the green S scrolls on the inner circle.

Make two open coils in each shade of green. These go from the side of the two-tone heart-shaped scroll, to the blue open coil.

Step 17.

Make two teardrops in each shade of both blue and green.

Place the shades of blue, point to point, next to the two-tone heart scrolls, and the two green at an angle on top of those, also point to point.

So for example, between spring and summer, spring blue on one side of the line, summer blue on the other. Spring green on one side, summer green on the other.

Step 18.

Roll two open coils in each shade of blue.

Unroll them so the tail will fit between the blue and green open coils on each side, meeting above the teardrops on the outside edge of the circle.

Step 19.

Create two teardrop coils and two tight coils in each shade of blue.

Decorate this section with teardrops on the tails and tight coils at the base where the tail meets the other open coils.

Step 20.

Add any extra decorations that you wish to finish off your design.

I hope you've enjoyed making your mandala, and taking your quilling journey through the seasons with me!

Your larger designs such as this one will look fantastic on display in a frame; it really adds the finishing touch. You can hang them proudly on your wall, or gift them to a loved one. Remember that when you buy a frame you will need the glass to be raised to accommodate your quilling. This type of frame is called either a deep box frame or a shadow box frame.

The more you quill, the more you will start to see the world in quilling shapes! I hope you have already felt the benefit of taking some time out for yourself, to sit and quill, slowing down for a moment to make something special. The satisfaction of seeing a finished design come together that YOU have created is really a feeling like no other, so do take a moment to savour that, and be proud of yourself!

Happy quilling,

Rachel x

Inspirational Gallery

The images in this section are by experienced members of the Quilling Guild and the Quirky Quillers collective. I hope that they provide further inspiration!

Above: *Urchin*, 2024, by Karl Stedman, made using 20cm diameter hand-rolled manipulated paper discs. © Karl Stedman

Right: A koi fish mandala by Shalu Krishan Gupta.
© Shalu Krishan Gupta

Below: A trio of seahorses created by Philippa Reid, using a combination of looped and coiled quilling techniques and set against a background of open ring coils.
© Philippa Reid

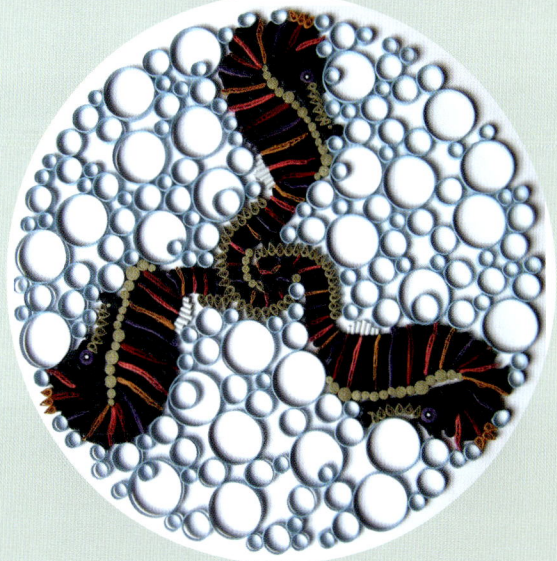

Above: *Goldfish Bowl*. This design came about as a way of using up all those tiny leftover bits of quilling paper; indeed they make for the perfect 'grit'! © Charlotte Darby

Above: *Scales and Fairy Tales.* Saul the Dragon was inspired by Anna Mercer's love of reading and anything fantastical. He was made using closed loose coils along with on-edge and beehive quilling techniques. © Anna Mercer

Below: *Bee and Summer Flowers* by Frances Marriott. Inspired by bees on passion flowers. Using 3 mm strips, the techniques included closed loose coil, comb and beehive. © Frances Marriott

Above: *Phoenix Rising* by Barbara Taylor. Growing from initial sketches, this developed into a mythical beast rising from the ashes, reflecting light and motion. Made using 3 mm metallic-edged strips and glass rhinestones, using traditional quilling techniques. © Barbara Taylor

Below: *Spring Blooms* by Janet Watling. The tree trunks and branches used the comb techinque. © Janet Watling

Above: Lance Corporal Derby XXXII, mascot of The Mercian Regimental Army and Derby Football club.
Created by Andrea Oram with Juya 3 mm quilling paper. © Andrea Oram

Templates

For several of the patterns in the book, you can copy one of these grey templates to quill directly onto, or copy one of the black templates for use on a lightbox.

Blossom Tree (see page 38).

Rainbow in the Clouds (see page 41).

Ice Cream Sundae (see page 57).

Dragonfly (see page 60).

Autumn (see page 74).

Toadstool (see page 81).

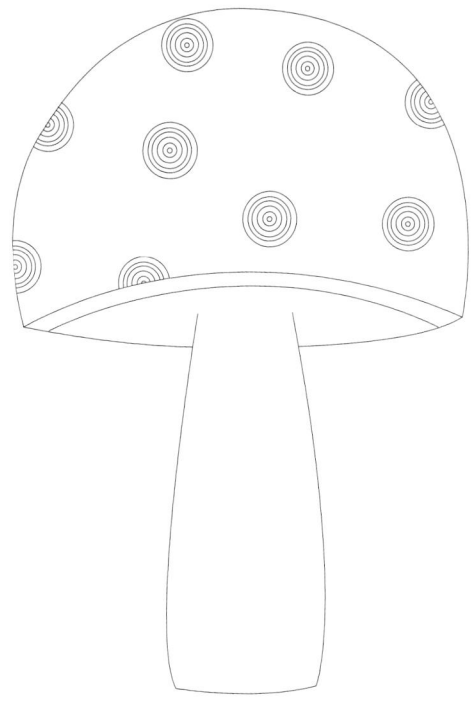

Pumpkin (see page 85).

Ice Skate (see page 103).

Mandala (see page 108).

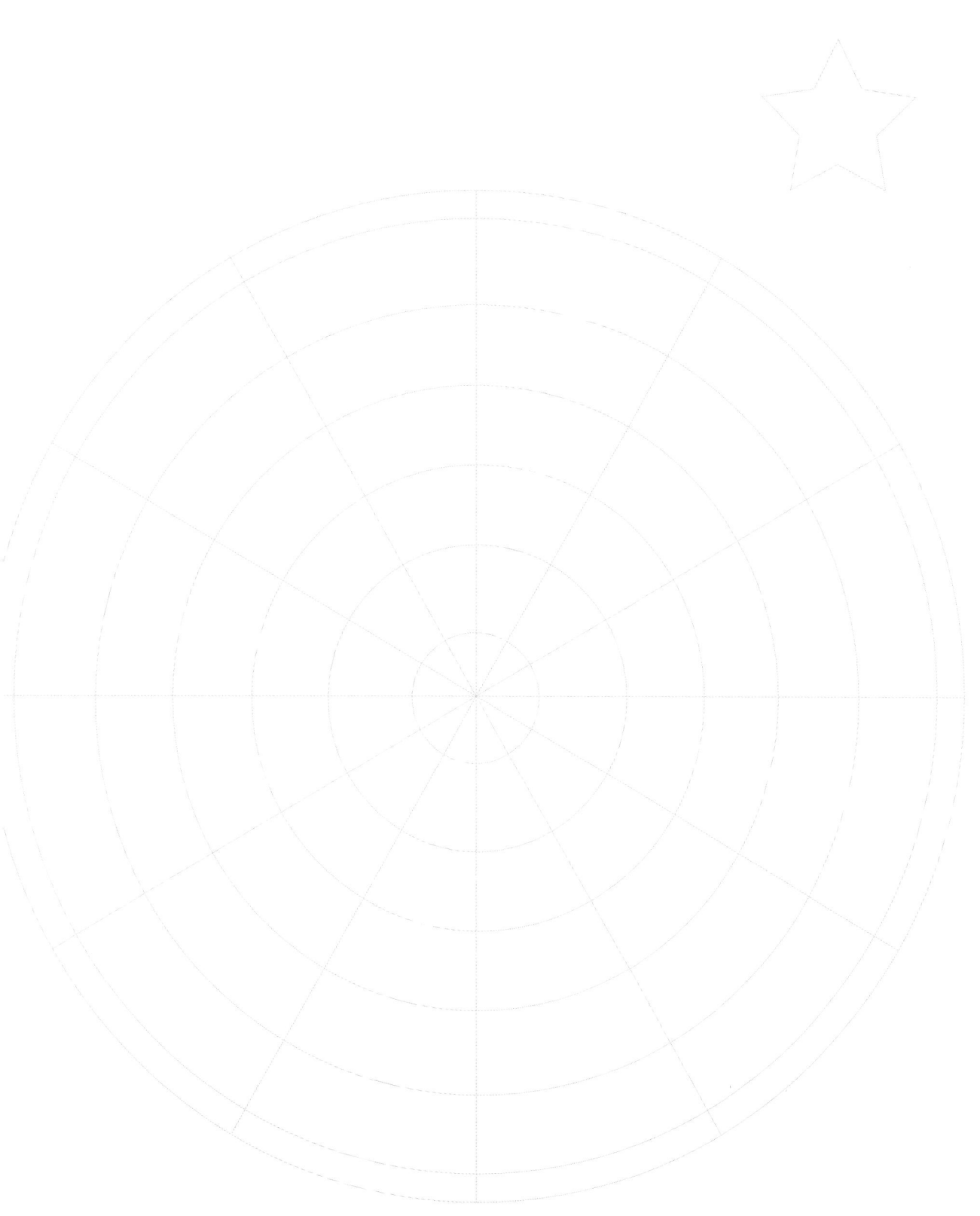

Suppliers and Further Information

UK

The Quirky Quillers
Online community, tutorials and inspiration.
www.thequirkyquillers.co.uk

Quilling Ascrollaway
Online quilling supplies.
www.quilling-ascrollaway.co.uk

PDQ Quilling
Online quilling supplies.
www.pdquilling.com

Hobbycraft
Online, plus stores nationwide. They have a
selection of deep box and shadow box frames in
different sizes.
www.hobbycraft.co.uk

The Range
A good selection of box frames – but be careful
which you choose as not all have raised glass.
www.therange.co.uk

USA

Quilled Creations
Online store.
www.quilledcreations.com

Hunter Creek Crafts
Online store.
www.huntercreekcrafts.com

Quilling Guilds

Quilling Guild
www.quilling-guild.weebly.com

North American Quilling Guild
www.naqg.org